Contents

Introduction

There are many skills which you will need to master in order to cope with the demands of day-to-day living. You need to know how to communicate with people, how to write letters, fill in forms, use telephone directories quickly and accurately. This book will teach you these and other important skills.

Book One has five Chapters and each Chapter has its own list of contents. These lists will give you a better idea of what the book is about. You will find them on pages 5, 29, 53, 73, and 95.

At the back of the book is an Index which you will find useful. If, for example, you have forgotten how to set out a letter, look up 'Letter Writing' in the Index and you will find the page which gives a letter layout.

At the end of each section of work, you will find marking instructions. Some work has answers given elsewhere in the book. Other work should be marked for you. Always try to mark your work or have it marked, as soon as you have finished it. If your answers are different from those in the book, make sure that you discuss them.

1 Headline news

Front-page headlines

READING This is the front page of the *Evening News*. A HEADLINE is missing from each numbered space. The headlines that fit into these spaces are on the next page.

Evening News

1

THE LEADER of one of the main steel unions hinted today that an end to the 10-week-old strike was in sight.

Hector Smith, general secretary of the National Union of Blastfurnacemen said: "I am optimistic, certainly more optimistic than last week."

Mr. Bill Sirs, leader of the Iron and Steel Trades Confederation, said it would be up to the two unions' executives to call off the strike.

This evening the union leaders seemed more hopeful of peace than at any time since the strike began. However, a note of caution was introduced by the strike coordinator Mr. Sandy Feather.

He said: "There is still a very long way to go. It would be wrong to raise hopes."

2

ROBERT REDFORD has been in London promoting his latest film *The Electric Horseman*. He ignored the photographers as he walked out to catch his flight home to America.

Then a young airline girl stepped in among the crowd and asked for "a couple of quick snaps".

Looking in the young lady's direction, he slowed down and smiled sweetly as she took some photos of her favourite star.

3

One passenger was killed and 17 others were hurt when a tourist bus crashed in Greece today.

Several Britons and Australians are believed to be among the injured.

Police said the coach careered off a main highway in Central Greece before rolling into a river below.

4

British Shipbuilders have won three major contracts worth £50 million, it was announced today.

The contracts, which will mean a job boost for the North East, Scotland and Northern Ireland, were won by the staff-owned company against fierce competition.

British Shipbuilders' marketing chief John Parker said: "This is a very good day for British shipbuilding."

See Page Six

See Page Nine

Missing headlines

1 Look at the numbered spaces on the front page of the *Evening News* (page 6). Then read the headlines on this page.
2 Write down the numbers 1–4 in your book, using a new line for each number. Next to each number write the headline which you think best fits that space.
3 Check your answers by reading the first sentence of each news story.

A
Britain wins £50m shipyard orders

B
Tourist bus in death crash

C
Steelmen 'optimistic' as the talks go on
IN THE MOOD FOR PEACE

D
Redford, polite to the last. . .

Record Catch in Thames and *Famous Head Lost* are two headlines which have stories printed elsewhere in the newspaper. These headlines are meant to catch your eye and to make you want to read the paper.

DISCUSSION

FAMOUS HEAD LOST

- Do you think this headline is about a missing headmaster? What else could it be about?

RECORD CATCH IN THAMES

- Is the story which follows this headline likely to be about a record landed from the River Thames by an angler? What else could the story be about?

Why is that headline there?

The editor of a newspaper chooses which stories are to be printed on the front page. Why do you think he chose those headlines numbered 1 to 4?

WRITING   You may need to turn back to page 6 and read the news stories before you write down the answers to these questions. Choose the best possible answers to each question from (a), (b), or (c). Write out the whole sentence.

1 IN THE MOOD FOR PEACE is the main headline because
    (a) It is the only front-page story which fits into that space on the page.
    (b) A possible end to a ten-week-old strike was the most important news of the day.
    (c) The *Evening News* is **anti-union** and wants to stop the strike.

2 REDFORD POLITE **TO THE LAST**... is a front page headline with a picture because
    (a) A famous filmstar makes interesting news and the picture **catches the reader's eye.**
    (b) The paper did not have any other pictures for the front page.
    (c) Robert Redford was **in the news** because he had been in London to promote his latest film.

3 TOURIST BUS IN DEATH CRASH — The fact that this headline is on the front page shows that
    (a) We have a **morbid** curiosity about disasters so papers make them front-page news.
    (b) There were some British and Australian people among the injured.
    (c) The bus driver had been **involved** in a similar crash before.

4 BRITAIN WINS £50m SHIPYARD ORDERS is a front-page headline since
    (a) This news item is small enough to fit into the last space on the page.
    (b) No-one expected the British yards to win the orders.
    (c) Work for British shipyards is **good news** for jobs and for exports.

5 FAMOUS HEAD LOST and **RECORD CATCH** IN THAMES — These two headlines without stories are put on the front page
    (a) To show readers that the *Evening News* is full of news.
    (b) To show readers that there are two interesting news **items** inside the paper.
    (c) To make readers so **curious** that they will want to buy the paper.

The answers are on page 13.

What does it mean?

Go back to the previous section — "Why is that headline there?"

WRITING Find the ten words or groups of words which are **in heavy print** and write each one down on a separate line. Head your work *LIST A*.
The correct meanings of the words are printed below in *LIST B*. Match the meanings from *LIST B* with the words in your *LIST A*.

LIST B.   (This is not in the same order as your *LIST A*.)
  1 unhealthy
  2 eager to learn more
  3 the most remarkable fishing achievement of its kind on record
  4 mixed up in
  5 attracts the reader's attention
  6 something that is being written about in the newspapers and talked about on radio and TV
  7 to the very end
  8 information which pleases the people who hear it
  9 being opposed to the union (Trades Union)
 10 pieces of news in a newspaper or on radio or TV

The answers are on page 13.

The story behind the headlines

READING An interesting newspaper story can be made eye-catching by a clever, funny or puzzling headline. Here are five headlines:

LIST A   The headlines
1 Nightmare Explosion
2 Drink and Ride Injures Three
3 High-Speed Love Match
4 Up from the Deep
5 Umbrella Power

WRITING Now look at *LIST B* which contains the five stories which go with these five headlines. Match the headline from *LIST A* with the correct story from *LIST B*.

LIST B   The stories
A A sunken boat has been raised to the surface of a canal by divers.
B An explosion ripped through a house in which a family was sleeping.
C A beauty queen married a racing driver in All Saints Church.
D Mrs Moore beats off robbers with her umbrella.
E A drunken motor-cyclist hurt three people when he crashed through a supermarket window.

The answers are on page 21.

Write your own!

Here are five more headlines. Think of five interesting or amusing stories that could go with them. Then write a few lines about each one.

1 Record Swim
2 Zoo Alert
3 Bank Mystery
4 Five Miles High
5 Carnival Triumph

Have your work marked.

Write a headline to go with this photograph. Then write the beginning of the story.

Four front-page stories

Here are four stories that are not quite ready for the front page of a newspaper.

First story – Drink and ride injures three

A youth, Gary Phillips, riding a Honda 250 motorcycle, crashed through the window of a High Street supermarket yesterday at 2.45 pm. He had been in a nearby pub at lunchtime where his mates dared him to drink ten pints of beer. Three shoppers were injured in the accident, one seriously. The injured shoppers and the motor-cyclist were taken to West Dene Hospital.

This is the beginning of the story. After the accident a reporter interviewed four people. What do you think each one said?

Jim (Gary's mate)

Mrs Phillips
(Gary's mother)

Supermarket
Manager

Mrs Harkouk
(injured in the accident)

WRITING Write down the actual words spoken by each person.

READING The newspaper will not print speech bubbles so the reporter will have to write out the actual words which were spoken by the four people he interviewed. Instead of speech bubbles the reporter will use "   " (speech marks) just before and just after the words spoken by each person. Here is an example.

Reporter   Gary

When our reporter asked, "Do you usually drink ten pints?" Gary replied, "No. I only did it because my mates dared me to."

"Do you usually drink 10 pints?"

"No. I only did it because my mates dared me to."

WRITING Look back at what you wrote down for the speech bubbles 1, 2, 3 and 4. Now use the same words to complete these sentences for the newspaper report. Use speech marks as in the example on page 12.

A At the scene of the accident, Gary's mate Jim said, ...

B When the Manager of the supermarket was asked what action he would take against the drunken motor-cyclist, he replied, ...

C At her home in Wisden Road, Mrs Phillips told the "News" reporter, ...

D That evening in hospital, Mrs Harkouk, one of the injured shoppers, moaned, ...

Have your work marked.

Conversation at the hospital

WRITING Here are five sentences. Write out each sentence putting in the speech marks, commas and question marks (if needed).

1 Tell me Doctor, will he ever walk again sobbed Gary's mother.

2 He'll be perfectly all right in a few days the doctor answered.

3 They're making a lot of fuss about nothing grumbled Gary.

4 How many times have I told you not to drink when you're driving shouted his mother.

5 I'll never do it again, Mum, honest he promised.

The answers are on page 23.

ANSWERS **Why is that headline there?** Questions on page 8.

1 (b)   2 (a)   3 (b)   4 (c)   5 (b)
If your answers were different from these, discuss them with your teacher or a friend.

ANSWERS **What does it mean?** Questions on page 9.

anti-union *9*	involved *4*
TO THE LAST *7*	good news *8*
catches the reader's eye *5*	RECORD CATCH *3*
in the news *6*	items *10*
morbid *1*	curious *2*

Conversation at the garage

READING The day after the accident, Gary went to Triku Garage where his bike had been taken for repair.

Gary: Good morning. I'm Gary Phillips. I've come about my bike.
Mechanic: Ah yes. Would that be the one brought in yesterday?
Gary: Yes. It's a red Honda 250.
Mechanic: Well I'm afraid it's going to need a lot of work done on it before you can ride it again.
Gary: Have you any idea how long it will take you?
Mechanic: Look, mate, I can't even start until the insurance people give me the go-ahead and they haven't been yet to inspect the damage.
Gary: Insurance? Oh . . . .

WRITING Continue this conversation between Gary and the mechanic. Write out the conversation using speech marks as you did for 1, 2, 3 and 4 on page 12. For instance, the first part of the conversation could be written like this:

"Good morning," said Gary. "I'm Gary Phillips. I've come about my bike."
"Ah yes. Would that be the one brought in yesterday?" asked the mechanic.

Other words that make writing a conversation more interesting are:

answered	argued	demanded	grumbled	mumbled
replied	shouted	whispered	promised	moaned
sobbed	suggested	muttered	screamed	laughed

Use some of these words in your conversation to show how Gary and the mechanic spoke to each other.

Have your work marked.

Second story – High-speed love match

Notes

READING Here are the notes for this story but they are not in the right order.

- Best man – well-known film star Graham Harvey
- Honeymoon – the island of Majorca
- Date of wedding – Saturday 21 June, All Saints Church 2.30
- Bridegroom – Cliff Taylor, British Grand Prix racing driver
- Bride's dress – white satin – lace veil and train – made by sister
- Going away car – vintage Rolls Royce
- Bride – Cheryl Stevens, Miss United Kingdom last year

WRITING This is the story of the wedding. Here are five sentences which need to be completed. Note that sentences *1, 2* and *4* have two gaps which need to be filled. Use the notes to fill in all the gaps then write out the story neatly on a piece of paper.

1 There was a large crowd at __ on __.
2 They had all come to see __ marry the famous and handsome __.
3 The bride was wearing a __.
4 After the ceremony, the bride and groom left the church in __ owned by the best man, __.
5 Miss Stevens said the married couple had planned a honeymoon __.

Research

Reporters have to be sure of their facts. If mistakes are printed in the newspaper all kinds of trouble may result. As the reporter who is writing up the *High-speed love match* story, you will need to find out what the following expressions mean:

1 *British Grand Prix racing driver.* Find out where and when Grand Prix races are held. Find out all you can about Mr Taylor's job.
2 *Lace veil and train.* Find out why some brides' dresses have trains and why nearly all brides wear veils.
3 *Vintage Rolls Royce.* 'Vintage', 'antique' and 'old' all mean the same. Or do they? Check the meanings of *vintage* and *antique* in a dictionary. Why isn't the Rolls Royce described as 'antique'?
4 *Miss United Kingdom.* The bride's name is Cheryl Stevens, not Miss United Kingdom. Why was she given this title? What is a beauty queen?

Have your work marked.

Third story – Nightmare explosion

This photograph was taken the morning after an explosion wrecked a house. Miraculously Mr and Mrs Powell and their children, Leon and Marcia, escaped alive. A reporter was sent to the scene of the explosion. He interviewed the two children.

"We were woken by a shattering bang. The house was shaking. Plaster covered my bed. We are lucky to be alive."

"I was shocked and dazed. As I staggered to the door, I stepped on a broken light bulb. There was blood everywhere. I nearly fainted."

READING The reporter wrote some notes in his notebook.

Family of four rescued after explosion - 2 am.

Neighbour raised the alarm.

Tykie - family dog - killed.

Family recently moved from St Lucia - buried in rubble over an hour.

Set free by firemen - taken to hospital by ambulance - not seriously injured.

Police have put up rope barrier to keep people away from danger - falling tiles and bricks.

Demolition and clean-up operation will begin when investigations by police and Gas Board are complete.

16

Take the place of the reporter; use *all* the information and write an exciting story that people will want to read.
Begin like this:

Nightmare explosion
Early yesterday morning, a family of four had a miraculous escape.

Have your work marked.

Crossword

Copy or trace the shape of the crossword. Then fill it in. The answers to the clues are in the story *Nightmare explosion* on page 16.

Clues across

1 Where the Powell family had moved from. (7 letters)
6 Marcia cut her foot on a broken _____ (4)
7 The ones who rescued the parents. (7)
9 A neighbour raised this. (5)
11 The huge noise that woke everyone up. (9)
12 Getting rid of the mess. A _____-up operation. (5)
13 The ones who did something to keep people away from danger. (6)

Clues down

2 The name of the family dog. (5)
3 The parents were buried in this. (6)
4 The vehicle which took the parents to hospital. (9)
5 The parents were _____ _____ by the firemen. (3, 4)
8 What was used to make the barrier to keep people away. (4)
10 The type of car on the right of the photograph. (4)

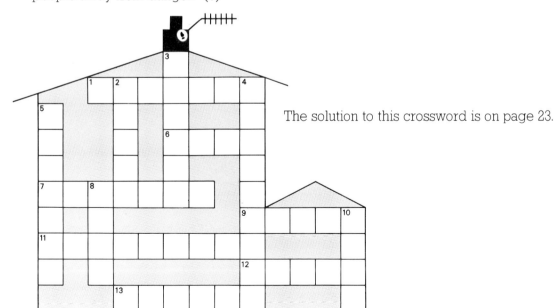

The solution to this crossword is on page 23.

Fourth story – Up from the deep

Dacorum Sub-Aqua Club came to the rescue of a sunken boat yesterday. The boat was a pleasure cruiser owned by Mrs Gwen Jones. It sank in the Grand Union Canal after it had been holed by vandals.

Now look at the following three pictures and the words that are printed beside them:

1

pump
suits
canvas
submerged
divers
hull
holes
bail
damaged
wrapped

2

forwards
pulled
barges
ropes
away
Sub-Aqua
tow
rescue
guided
canal

3

water
seeped
fastened
Land Rover
boards
towed
heavy
sinking
line
haul

Fill in the missing words

WRITING Write down the word which best fits into each space. Choose the words from the lists beside the pictures on these two pages.

1 When the ___ had put on their wet ___ and face masks they examined the ___ of the ___ boat. They found several ___ in the rear section of the boat which they sealed up with strips of ___. Then they ___ a large tarpaulin around the ___ area. With the help of a powerful ___ the water was then pumped out of the boat. To speed up this process, a volunteer began to ___ out water with a plastic bucket.

2 The next stage of the ___ operation was to ___ the pleasure cruiser along the ___ to a point where it could be ___ up onto the bank. Several ___ were tied to secure fittings on the boat. Then, while some members of the ___ Club hauled the boat ___, two divers in the water kept the boat ___ from the bank and ___ it around the ___ tied up at the side of the canal.

3 The cruiser was too ___ to be pulled up onto the bank so the rescue team put a strong ___ around the boat and ___ this to a ___ ___. Then they pumped out the ___ that had ___ into the boat while it was being ___ along the canal. The Land Rover then started to ___ the cruiser up out of the water and ___ were placed under the hull to stop it ___ into the soft bank.

Write down your ending to this story in a few sentences.

Have your work marked.

Grand Union Canal

People sailing on the canals use maps to tell them where they can buy food or fuel, where the locks are and other things they may need to know.

WRITING Look carefully at this map and then write the answers to the six questions.

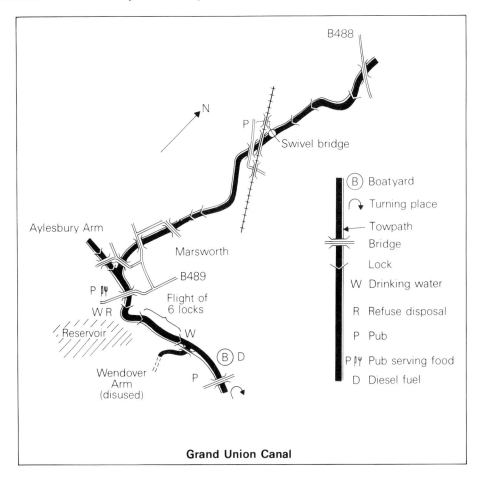

Grand Union Canal

1 If you were sailing from the pub below the Wendover Arm to the Aylesbury Arm Junction, what would you see? List everything in the order in which you would see it and say whether it would be on your right or your left.
2 How many bridges cross the section of the canal shown on the map?
3 Why do you think a number of locks close together is called a "flight of locks"?
4 If you were moored outside the pub which serves food, facing west, and you wanted to turn the boat round, where could you best do it?
5 What crosses the canal between the pub and the Swivel Bridge?
6 Look at the services shown on the map. Why do you think a canal journey needs to be planned?

The answers are on page 23.

Life afloat

READING Read this extract about living conditions on the canals a hundred years ago.

A casual glance at a narrow boat gaily painted with roses and castles, as it passed slowly through the English countryside, could easily leave the impression that the life of the canal boatman was one long holiday. This was very far from the truth; the work was extremely hard at times, and the boatmen and their families often worked long hours, seven days a week. The only comfort during bad winter weather was a small coal-burning range inside the cabin that was the boatman's home.

The number of people allowed to live in a narrow boat cabin was strictly limited. The number varied according to the size of the cabin, but was usually three adults or two adults and a child. It was possible, in a cabin allowed by law to accommodate three people, for an extra person to sleep on the floor, while in the second cabin three children could sleep in the main bed, one on the side bed and one on the floor, making a total of five in all. The engine room of the motor boat was sometimes used to relieve overcrowding, with one child sleeping each side of the engine.

from *Life Afloat* by Robert Wilson

Match beginnings with endings

WRITING Now complete these four sentences by finding the right ending for each and writing the whole sentence in your book.

1 The boatmen and their families
2 The only comfort during bad weather
3 The number of people allowed to
   live in a narrow boat cabin
4 The engine room of the motor boat

was used to relieve overcrowding.
often worked long hours, seven
days a week.
was a small coal-burning range.
was strictly limited.

The answers are on page 28.

ANSWERS **The story behind the headlines** Questions on page 10.

1 B   *2 E*   *3 C*   *4 A*   *5 D*

Wordshapes

If you draw an outline around the words *read and think* you get this shape:

Umbrella power

Now read this story and fill in the shapes in the sentences after it.

Umbrella power

ARMED only with her plain black umbrella, Susanna Moore (right) beat two masked raiders of a sub-post office and forced one of them into submission. "I just sort of clobbered him with the brolly. It was as simple as that," she said modestly.

Mrs Moore was one of nine people presented with Post Office bravery awards in London yesterday. She received a cheque for £100 in recognition of her action in forcing the robbers to drop the £235 they had forced from the assistant at the Shenley sub-post office at Radlett, Hertfordshire.

Another special award of £75 went yesterday to a 74-year-old sub-postmaster, Mr Edward Rogers, who foiled a raid by three youths on his sub-post office at Ivychurch, Romney Marsh, Kent, by grabbing a large poker and setting his dog on the raiders when they demanded money. They lost their nerve and fled, but were subsequently arrested.

WRITING Complete these sentences. The words you need to find are all in the story.

1 Mrs Moore was armed with an ⬚⬚⬚⬚⬚⬚⬚.

2 The two people she beat were ⬚⬚⬚⬚⬚⬚ ⬚⬚⬚⬚⬚⬚⬚.

3 The place they were trying to rob was a ⬚⬚⬚⬚ ⬚⬚⬚⬚⬚⬚.

4 Mrs Moore spoke about what she had done very ⬚⬚⬚⬚⬚⬚⬚⬚.

5 Nine courageous people received ⬚⬚⬚⬚⬚⬚⬚ ⬚⬚⬚⬚⬚⬚.

6 Mrs Moore received a ⬚⬚⬚⬚⬚⬚ for £100.

7 The award given to Mr Rogers was a ⬚⬚⬚⬚⬚⬚⬚ one.

8 The quick action of Mr Rogers prevented or ⬚⬚⬚⬚⬚⬚ the raid.

9 He attacked the raiders with a ⬚⬚⬚⬚⬚ ⬚⬚⬚⬚.

10 After they had lost their ⬚⬚⬚⬚⬚ the ⬚⬚⬚⬚⬚⬚ were ⬚⬚⬚⬚⬚⬚⬚ by the police.

The answers are on page 28.

Conversation at the hospital Questions on page 13.

1 "Tell me Doctor, will he ever walk again?" sobbed Gary's mother.
2 "He'll be perfectly all right in a few days," the doctor answered.
3 "They're making a lot of fuss about nothing," grumbled Gary.
4 "How many times have I told you not to drink when you're driving," shouted his mother.
5 "I'll never do it again, Mum, honest." he promised.

Solution to crossword on page 17.

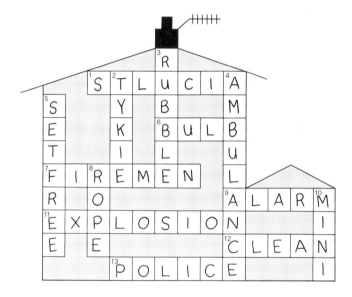

Grand Union Canal Questions on page 20.

1 You would see:
   a boatyard (right), the disused Wendover Arm (left), a place for taking on water (right), flight of 6 locks, reservoir (left), a place for water and rubbish (left), a road (B489) which crosses the canal by a bridge (left and right), a pub which serves food (left).
2 Ten bridges are shown.
3 The locks are designed to take a boat from one level to another, like a staircase.
4 You would turn at the junction of the Aylesbury Arm with the Grand Union Canal.
5 A railway line crosses the canal here.
6 Although the map shows two water points which are quite close together, there is only one place where fuel can be bought. Most boats run on diesel fuel, so a journey needs to be planned in advance.

The hand!

DISCUSSION Look at the picture on the opposite page. Then talk about these questions.

- What can you see?
- Is the hand a left or a right hand?
- Whose hand might it be?
- Why is it reaching out?
- What position is the rest of the body in?
- Does the photograph show smoke or fog?
- What could happen very soon?

WRITING Write a story suitable for a newspaper to go with this photograph. Give it a title. You could start your story like this:

> *There was a muffled sound of coughing. The door swung open and a hand appeared. It seemed to be groping through the smoke.*

Have your work marked.

Lightning cure for blind man

Read this story.

LIGHTNING CURE FOR BLIND MAN

A 62-year-old man, blinded in an accident nine years ago, regained his sight after he was struck by lightning near his home in Falmouth, Maine, his wife said yesterday.

Doctors confirmed that Edwin Robinson, a former truck driver, could see for the first time since he became blind as the result of a road accident.

Mr Robinson was knocked to the ground by lightning on Wednesday when he took shelter under a tree during a thunderstorm. His wife said he could also now hear without his hearing aid.—A.P.

WRITING Here are three lists of words. Write out the five complete sentences by matching a beginning from *LIST A* with a middle from *LIST B* and an ending from *LIST C*. The answers are all in the newspaper story.

LIST A	*LIST B*	*LIST C*
1 A 62-year-old man	he could also now hear	could see for the first time since he became blind.
2 Edwin Robinson	was knocked to the ground by lightning	without his hearing aid.
3 Mr Robinson	a former truck driver	near his home in Falmouth.
4 His wife said	by lightning	when he took shelter under a tree.
5 He was struck	blinded in an accident	regained his sight.

The answers are on page 28.

Write a letter

Imagine that you are Mr or Mrs Robinson. Write a letter to your brother or sister telling them the good news and inviting them to a family celebration.

Producing your own newspaper

Stage one: Planning

1 The group must decide who the paper will be for. Will it be for a particular age group, for people in a certain area, for people who share similar interests or for anybody?

2 Find out what the people who are going to buy the paper want to read. One way to do this is to carry out a survey amongst the people who will buy the paper. Prepare a sheet like this:

	Name Anansi Age 14	Name Tony Age 15	Name Age	Name Age
Do you want .... ?				
Just local news		✓		
Stories (fiction) as well as news	✓			
Sports reports				
Which sports	Athletics	Football		
Entertainment information	✓	✓		
Puzzles and crosswords	✓	✓		
Jokes		✓		
Letters	✓			
Adverts	✓	✓		
Anything else	Fashion	Hobbies		

Two columns have been filled in as examples.

3 Study the results of your survey. Make a list of the replies starting at the most popular items and going down to the least popular items.

4 Decide how much space is going to be given to each item or section in the paper.

Stage two: Writing and designing

1 Collect information, news, interviews, pictures, drawings, and so on, for each section.

2 Write out and arrange each section as it will appear on each page of the paper.

3 Make sure each page is interesting to read and look at.

4 Avoid putting too much on a page so that it looks overcrowded or untidy.

5 Choose a title for your paper.

Stage three: Printing and selling

1 Find out what printing methods are available.

2 How many copies are you going to print?

3 How much will each method cost?

4 Choose the best one for your paper.

5 Fix a price for each copy.

Life afloat Questions on page 21.

1 The boatmen and their families often worked long hours, seven days a week.
2 The only comfort during bad weather was a small coal-burning range.
3 The number of people allowed to live in a narrow boat cabin was strictly limited.
4 The engine room of the motor boat was used to relieve overcrowding.

Umbrella power Questions on page 22.

1 umbrella
2 masked raiders
3 post office
4 modestly
5 bravery awards

6 cheque
7 special
8 foiled
9 large poker
10 nerve, raiders, arrested

Lightning cure for blind man Questions on page 26.

1 A 62-year-old man, blinded in an accident, regained his sight.
2 Edwin Robinson, a former truck driver, could see for the first time since he became blind.
3 Mr Robinson was knocked to the ground by lightning when he took shelter under a tree.
4 His wife said he could also now hear without his hearing aid.
5 He was struck by lightning near his home in Falmouth.

2 Sending messages

Clear instructions

READING "Cut off a metre of that for me, Dave, then smooth down the ends with sandpaper. Be quick about it because I want to finish the job before we knock off at 5.30. Now be careful about the measurement because that is the only piece of wood in the store suitable for the job."

The foreman handed me a three metre length of pine panelling. This was my first unsupervised task so I was determined to follow the foreman's instructions carefully. He had said a metre so I sawed off a metre and a quarter just to be sure and to allow for any mistakes. I wasn't satisfied with the first piece so I cut off another piece exactly one metre long. Twenty minutes later, the foreman came in as I was putting the finishing touches to the sandpapering.

"You . . . idiot! Can't you understand clear instructions? I asked for exactly two metres of panelling and what am I left with? Three useless bits I can't do anything with!"

Beginnings and endings

WRITING Read the beginning of each sentence on the left then find the right ending from the list on the right. When you have made the correct match, write the complete sentence in your book.

BEGINNINGS
1 The foreman wanted
2 Dave thought he wanted
3 As it was his first unsupervised task
4 The first piece of panelling cut was
5 The foreman was left with

ENDINGS
A Dave followed the instructions carefully
B a piece of panelling two metres long.
C three useless pieces of wood.
D one metre and a quarter long.
E a piece of panelling one metre long.

The answers are on page 36.

Find the right word

READING Read this passage. This is what the foreman should have said to Dave. Ten words have been left out, one from each gap.

The foreman said, "Come here, Dave. I've got a _____ for you. Here's the _____ piece of pine panelling we have in _____. It's three metres long. I want you to measure off and cut a piece _____ two metres long. You can put the _____ over piece back in the store. Oh, you'll need to get some _____ too because I want the edges _____ smooth. Do you think you can manage that without any _____? I think you can and that is why I am willing to _____ you with this _____"

WRITING Now write out the whole passage, filling in the ten gaps with the best words from this list of fifteen words.

LIST A

assistance	sandpaper	unsupervised	only	trust
job	task	perfectly	left	exactly
store	allow	complete	last	precisely

Discuss your answers with a member of your group.

Find the hidden word

Five words from *LIST A* are hidden in this word puzzle. Copy the puzzle on your paper. Then find all the letters in the first word which is *UNSUPERVISED*, and put a line through each letter of the word as you find it in the puzzle. Do the same for these words:

PRECISELY   TASK
ASSISTANCE   COMPLETE

Then look at the remaining letters. They form a word which is also on *LIST A*. Write the word on your paper.

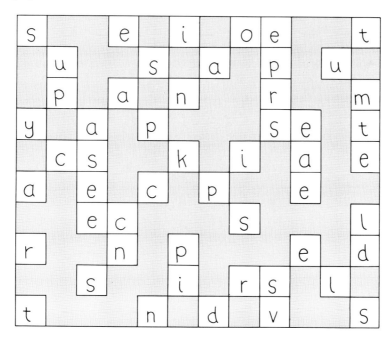

The answer is on page 36.

Giving clear directions

WRITING Look at the map of New Town. Find the Railway Station, the Post Office and the Motorway Service Area. Write down directions for the following short journeys.

1 From the Railway Station
(a) give directions to a motorist who is going from the station to the Swimming Pool.
(b) give directions to a person who wants to walk from the station to the Library by the shortest possible route.

2 From the Post Office
(a) give directions to a person who wants to walk from the Post Office to the Cinema by the shortest possible route.
(b) give directions to a motorist who wants to drive from the Post Office to Tower Court Luxury Flats.

3 From the Motorway Service Area
Give directions to a motorist who wants to drive from the Service Area to
(a) the Bowling Alley Car Park
(b) the Police Station.

Map quiz

Look carefully at the map of New Town. Write down the answers to these questions.

1 What is directly across the road from the Bus Station?
2 What is on the corner opposite the Church where Jubilee Road meets North Street?
3 If your car broke down in the Cinema Car Park, describe the simplest route you could take to the nearest garage.
4 After leaving the Disco late at night, where would you go to find a taxi to take you home?
5 What important public services are in both Spring Lane and North Street?
6 If you only wanted to buy goods in the Market, where would you park your car?
7 If you were driving from Jubliee Road into North Street and heading for the Cinema via South Street, in what order would you pass the following buildings?

Garage	Bowling Alley	Bus Station
Leisure Centre	Tower Court Flats	Disco Dance Hall
Banks	Swimming Pool	Coach Station

8 You left a parcel on a bus. You go to the Coach Station Lost Property Office by mistake. How would they direct you to the right Lost Property Office?

Check your answers with your friends.

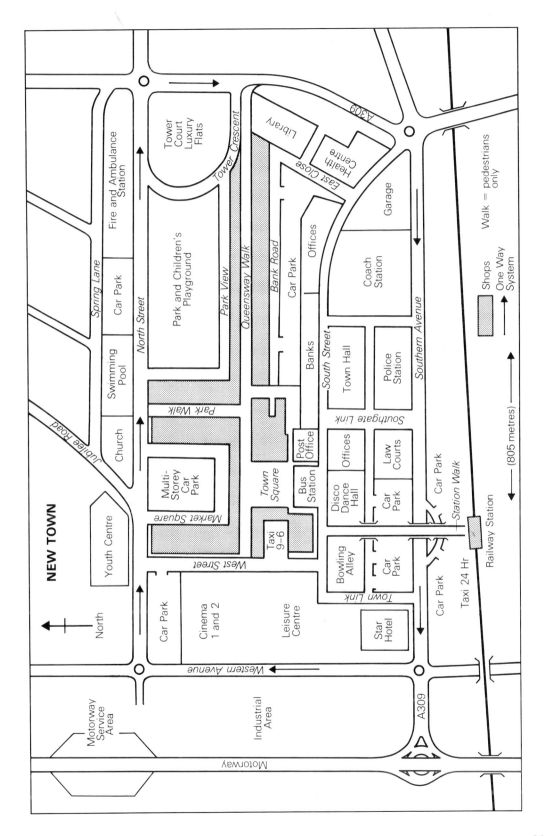

NEW TOWN

North

Motorway Service Area

Motorway

Industrial Area

Jubilee Road

Spring Lane

Youth Centre

Car Park

Cinema 1 and 2

Leisure Centre

Western Avenue

Star Hotel

Church

Swimming Pool

Car Park

Fire and Ambulance Station

North Street

Park View

Park Walk

Multi-Storey Car Park

Market Square

West Street

Town Square

Taxi 9-6

Park and Children's Playground

Tower Court Luxury Flats

Tower Crescent

Queensway Walk

Bank Road

Car Park

Offices

East Close

Library

Health Centre

A309

Garage

Coach Station

Banks

South Street

Post Office

Bus Station

Town Hall

Offices

Disco Dance Hall

Car Park

Law Courts

Southgate Link

Police Station

Southern Avenue

Car Park

Station Walk

Bowling Alley

Car Park

Town Link

Car Park

Taxi 24 Hr

Railway Station

A309

(805 metres)

Shops

One Way System

Walk = pedestrians only

33

Messages by telephone

Frying squad

READING

Copper's *takeaway* breakfast *cereal* went on and on . . . .

Two policemen got more than they *bargained for* when they collected a 60p breakfast for a prisoner.

A cafe *misheard* their order over the telephone . . . . and served up SIXTY steaming helpings of sausage, egg and toast.

They filled *half-a-dozen* carrier bags and left the *bemused* policemen facing a bill of £36.00.

The *slap-up* mistake started when *PCs* Mike Edwards and Brian Davies from New Town were told to get a prisoner's breakfast because the station *canteen* was closed.

They ordered the meal from a motorway cafe two miles away from New Town, then drove off to pick it up.

PC Edwards said, "We couldn't believe our eyes when we saw the food. We explained that we'd ordered ONE 60p breakfast and not sixty breakfasts. Finally we got away with paying for just the one meal." But the troubles of the two-man "frying squad" were not over yet. When they arrived back at the station, they found the breakfast wasn't even wanted. The prisoner had been *bailed* while they were away.

WRITING Write the answers to these questions. Use the information in the passage.

1 Why did the police have to send out an order for a breakfast?
2 What was the breakfast that was ordered?
3 How far away was the motorway cafe from the police station?
4 Why were the policemen surprised when they reached the motorway cafe?
5 Why was their journey a waste of time?

Turn to page 37 for the answers.

Now answer these questions. You will not find the answers in the passage. Work out the best possible answers after reading the passage again.

6 Why did the police order the breakfast from a *motorway* cafe?
7 Why did not one of the "frying squad" policemen cook the breakfast in the station?
8 Why did the cafe prepare sixty breakfasts instead of one 60p breakfast? Whose fault was it?
9 Why were *two* policemen sent to collect the breakfast?
10 What is funny about the headline "Frying Squad"?

Discuss your last five answers with a friend.

Word meanings

Look back at the passage headed "Frying squad" on page 34. Ten words or groups of words are printed in italics.

WRITING First write the words on paper, a new line for each item. Next to the words write their correct meanings taken from the list below.

NOTE: Use your dictionary to check meanings unless you are absolutely sure of them.

1 excellent
2 heard something incorrectly
3 a restaurant in a factory or office building
4 a shop where cooked meals are bought and taken away to be eaten
5 Police Constables
6 were prepared for
7 let free until tried, on payment of money to a court of law
8 six (half of twelve)
9 completely puzzled and confused
10 food made from grain, especially eaten at breakfast

When you have finished, turn to page 44 for the answers.

Same sound, different meaning – Part 1

READING The headline *Frying Squad* is funny because it should really be Flying Squad. It is a play on words (a pun). Sometimes you hear words which have a similar sound but mean different things. Here is an example:

$$63 + 22 = 85 \checkmark \boxed{\text{right}} \qquad \text{Dear So,} = \boxed{\text{write}}$$

WRITING The words in *LIST A* sound the same as the words in *LIST B*, but the letters of the words in *LIST B* are jumbled up. Unjumble the letters and write out both words side by side.

EXAMPLE flour   lefowr   *becomes*   flour   flower

LIST A	*LIST B*
for	rouf
here	reah
knows	sone
one	own
pear	riap
piece	apece
sale	lasi
sun	ons
weak	kewe
where	awer
wood	douwl

Turn to page 44 for the answers.

Turn to page 44 for the answers.

ANSWERS **Beginnings and endings** Questions on page 30.

1 B   2 E   3 A   4 D   5 C

ANSWERS **Find the hidden words** Questions on page 31.

SANDPAPER

Match the word with the definition

Each word on the left can be matched with a definition on the right. Write down a word then write the correct definition after it.

WORDS   *DEFINITIONS*
check   A feeling of suffering or discomfort in a particular part of the body.
cheque   Several neat lines of people, chairs or other things side by side.
cue   A particular spot or area.
queue   To stop or control something. An examination to make certain that
          something is correct.
pain   A flat sea fish which can be eaten.
pane   A line of waiting people, cars, etc.
place   Any of various bushes with strong, prickly stems, divided leaves, and often
          sweet-smelling flowers. The flower of this bush.
plaice   A specially printed order form to a bank to pay money.
rose   A single sheet of glass for use in a frame, especially of a window.
rows   A long, straight, wooden rod, slightly thicker at one end than the other,
          used for striking a ball in billiards, snooker, etc.

When you have finished, check your answers with a dictionary. Your dictionary definitions may have a slightly different wording.

ANSWERS **Frying squad** Questions on page 35.

1 The police had to send out an order for breakfast because the station canteen was closed.
2 The breakfast ordered was for sausage, egg and toast.
 or
 The order was for a breakfast costing 60p.
3 The motorway cafe was two miles from the police station.
4 The policemen were surprised because they were given sixty breakfasts, not one at 60p.
5 The journey was a waste of time because when the policemen returned to the station, the prisoner for whom the breakfast had been ordered had been bailed out.

Same sound, different meaning – Part 2

WRITING Here are four pairs of sentences which have underlined words. These words look different and have different meanings but sound the same. Look at each pair and answer the question below it. Write your answers on paper.

1 Is there a <u>cue</u> in the billiard room?
  Is there a <u>queue</u> in the billiard room?
  Which word means "a line of people"?

2 I don't <u>know</u>.
  I don't. <u>No</u>.
  Which word means "to have information"?

3 I'll ask. He's in the <u>wood</u>.
  I'll ask him if he <u>would</u>.
  Which word means "a place where trees grow"?

4 Can you <u>hear</u>?
  Can you? <u>Here</u>.
  Which word means "this place"?

Now here are six pairs of sentences, each with a picture. Look at the picture. Read the two sentences, (a) and (b), and write the correct sentence on paper.

5 (a) Would you like a pear?
  (b) Would you like a pair?

6 (a) Who are these for?
  (b) Who are these four?

7 (a) I waited for two long poles.
  (b) I waited for too long.

8 (a) Can you see water?
  (b) Can you drink sea water?

9 (a) Just right! You turn left here.   You turn
  (b) Just write, "You turn left here."   Left here

10 (a) They're here.
   (b) There or here?

The answers are on page 44.

Choose the spelling that fits the meaning

WRITING Write out the following sentences. Where there are words in brackets choose the one word which fits the meaning of the sentence. You may want to check the meaning in a dictionary.

 1 I bought a (blew, blue) coat in the closing down (sale, sail).
 2 I remembered to buy (your, you're) jeans while I was (there, their).
 3 The shop delivered this parcel (four, for) you an (hour, our) ago.
 4 The van driver wasn't (to, too, two) sure if this was the right (plaice, place).
 5 (Wood, Would) you ask him to deliver this to the (right, write) house?
 6 Did you (by, bye, buy) me a pound of (pairs, pears) and two pounds (of, off) apples?
 7 (No, Know) there was a long (cue, queue) outside the greengrocer's.
 8 It's all right, (wheel, we'll) get them next (week, weak).
 9 (Eye, I) shall have to go to the bank. Is there (one, won) near (here, hear)?
10 Oh! When (yew, you) go, (would, wood) you cash me a (check, cheque) for £20?

When you have finished, turn to page 47 for the answers.

Picture clues puzzle

Write out the following sentences filling in the missing words, one in each sentence. A drawing suggests the sound of the missing word but the spelling is different. Make sure you get the right spelling.

 1 This week there is a 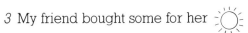 at the clothes shop.

 2 Socks are reduced if you buy four

 3 My friend bought some for her

 4 I believe this parcel is 4 you.

 5 Would you put that parcel over

 6 He always the answers to the questions.

 7 I can never get them Can you?

 8 You'd think he know that by now.

Turn to page 47 for the answers.

Telephone conversation – Crossed lines

READING Mrs Stockly is telephoning a clothes shop to find out if they are selling children's socks in a sale that has been advertised in the local paper.

At the same time Mrs Perry is telephoning a greengrocer to give him an order for fruit and vegetables which she wants delivered to her house.

During these two telephone conversations the lines become crossed. This means that sometimes Mrs Stockly is talking to the greengrocer when she thinks she is talking to the shop assistant in the clothes shop, and Mrs Perry is sometimes talking to the shop assistant when she thinks she is talking to the greengrocer.

Mrs Stockly dials the telephone number of the clothes shop. The telephone rings. A shop assistant answers the telephone.

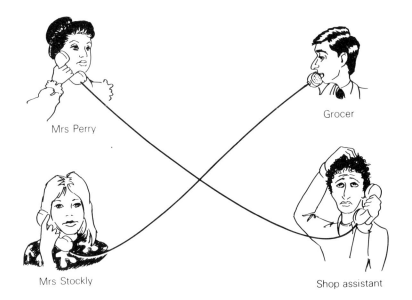

Mrs Perry

Grocer

Mrs Stockly

Shop assistant

  Assistant: Hello. Better Ware Clothes Limited.
Mrs Stockly: Hello. Do you have any children's socks in your sale this week?
  Assistant: I'll ask for you. Wait a moment please.

Meanwhile, Mrs Perry has telephoned the greengrocer.

   Grocer: Hello. Fruit and Flower Family Greengrocer.
 Mrs Perry: Hello. May I place an order for some fruit and vegetables please?
   Grocer: Certainly madam. What would you like?
 Mrs Perry: I'd like half-a-dozen pears please.

At this moment the lines become crossed.

  Assistant: Hello.
 Mrs Perry: Hello. Do you have any pears?
  Assistant: Yes, we have a large number of pairs in our sale.

Mrs Perry: Are they green or yellow?

Assistant: Both green and yellow. You can even have ones with stripes on if you like.

Mrs Perry: No, I think I'll have yellow ones. I want them for my son's birthday.

Assistant: What size would you like, madam?

Mrs Perry: Whatever size you have as long as they're not bruised.

The lines become crossed.

Mrs Stockly: Hello. Do you have any pairs?

Grocer: Of course, Madam. You wanted half-a-dozen, didn't you?

Mrs Stockly: No, only four. Two pairs for my son and two pairs for my daughter. They get through them so quickly. But they must have them for school.

Grocer: Well, I could sort out some smaller ones for you. Then you could have six small pears for the price of four larger pears. Would that help?

Mrs Stockly: No, it wouldn't. My children must have large pairs, otherwise their feet ache.

The lines become crossed

Assistant: (*sounding puzzled*) Did you say bruised, Madam?

Mrs Stockly: No, I said ache. Have you got four large pairs?

Assistant: Yellow ones, wasn't it?

Mrs Stockly: No, grey ones with elasticated tops.

Assistant: As you wish, Madam. We have a good selection of grey pairs. Was there anything else you wanted to ask about?

The lines become crossed.

Mrs Perry: Do you think if I bought the pears today, they would last until Saturday?

Assistant: Of course, Madam. Our produce is of the best quality. If you wanted to pay a little bit more you could buy an indestructible pair.

Mrs Perry: Really? I've not heard of those. How much are they?

Assistant: 85 pence a pair.

Mrs Perry: 85 pence a pear! That's far too much. I'll have the ordinary ones.

The lines become crossed.

Assistant: Is there anything else you would like to know, Madam?

Mrs Stockly: Yes, do you have any white cricket trousers? I believe they're called cricket whites.

Assistant: Yes, Madam, we have cricket whites too.

Mrs Stockly: No, not two, just one.

The lines become crossed.

Grocer: Will there be anything else, Madam?

Mrs Perry: Yes, I'd better have some potatoes. What do you recommend?

Grocer: Well, the whites are a very good quality and they are a few pence cheaper.

Mrs Perry: Well, you've convinced me.

The lines become crossed.

Grocer: You'd like some whites then?

Mrs Stockly: Yes. They are really white, aren't they? I don't want them if they are a dull cream. What is their exact colour?

Grocer: Well, they're a sort of muddy brown at the moment. But they'll come up white if you scrape them and scrub them well.

The lines become crossed.

Mrs Perry: I'd better have some whites then.

Assistant: What size?

Mrs Perry: Oh give me big ones will you. My boys love cutting them up into chips.

Assistant: How much would you like . . . . .

Mrs Perry: (*interrupting before the Assistant can say, "How much would you like to pay for them?"*)

About 14 pounds please.

Assistant: What a coincidence! They are exactly £14.00.

Mrs Perry: That's lovely. Would you like my name and address so that you know where to send my order?

The lines become crossed.

Mrs Stockly: Are you open till late this evening? I would like to come and see the items we have been talking about.

Grocer: There is no need, Madam. I'll bring them round to your house. May I have your name and address, please?

DISCUSSION Discuss how this play could end. Then write out a possible ending to the play using as many crossed lines as you like. You can include what is said when the Grocer and the van driver from Better Ware deliver the goods to the addresses they have been given.

When you have finished, read through your play or record it with a few friends.

Using a telephone

Telephone message

READING When Bill Winters arrived home, he saw this message next to the telephone:

Bill, ring Evans about boots. Margaret

Bill looked up Evans in the telephone directory. This is what he saw:

Evans Andrew B, 55 Newlands Road . . .**Worton** 51732
Evans Alan E, 77 Station Road . . . .**Bucknold** 46914
Evans Dr A.M, Health Centre
   (Appointments) . . . .**Clapton** 72839
Evans Dr A.M, 4 Keats Way . . . .**Clapton** 72551
Evans, B.D,
   196 Alexandra Road . . . .**New Town** 60437
Evans, B.R, Shoe Repairs,
   73 High Street, ...**New Town** 63998
Evans, C.J, 39 Alison Road . . . .**Yetford** 81722
Evans C.J, 103 Crofton Road . . . .**Grumpton** 4715
Evans David N, Oak Tree Farm,
   Stotfold . . . .**Ickfield** 3025
Evans David R,
   25 Spring Terrace . . . .**New Town** 60047
Evans D.V, 10 Church Street . . . .**Bucknold** 41752

Bill dialled New Town 60437. This is the telephone conversation that followed:

B. D. Evans: Hello. New Town 60437.
        Bill: Hello. My wife asked me to ring you up about the boots.
B. D. Evans: Oh, you've got the wrong number. You want B. R. Evans, the shoe repairer in the High Street. I'm B. D. Evans.
        Bill: I'm very sorry to have troubled you.
B. D. Evans: Don't worry. It often happens. Goodbye.
        Bill: Thanks. Goodbye.

WRITING Answer these questions.

1 What number should Bill have rung?
2 Why do you think he rang the wrong number?
3 Who would he probably have spoken to if he had rung Yetford 81722?
4 The message was written in such a way that it was not very helpful. Write out the message for Bill so that it is completely clear.

Check your answers with your friends.

How to find the telephone number you want

READING Follow these guidelines:

1 Find the *SURNAME*
Surnames are printed in alphabetical order.

Esmond . . .
Euston . . .
Evans . . .
Evanson . . .

2 Find the *INITIALS*
People with the same surnames are in alphabetical order of initials.

Evans A, . . .
Evans A. E, . . .
Evans A. M, . . .
Evans B. D, . . .

Where the forename or first name is printed, the order is decided only by the alphabetical order of the initials.

Evans Andrew B, . . .
Evans Alan E, . . .
Evans Adam M, . . .

3 Find the *ADDRESS*
People with the same surname and initials are in alphabetical order of address. Look at the name of the road, not the number.

Evans C. J, 39 Alison Rd . . .
Evans C. J, 22 Beech Drive . . .
Evans C. J, 103 Crofton Rd . . .

(For more information, see inside the front cover of a Telephone Directory.)

ANSWERS **Word meanings** Questions on page 35.

takeaway (4)	bemused (9)
cereal (10)	slap-up (1)
bargained for (6)	PCs (5)
misheard (2)	canteen (3)
half-a-dozen (8)	bailed (7)

ANSWERS **Same sound, different meaning – Part 1** Questions on page 36.

four, hear, nose, won, pair, peace, sail, son, week, wear, would.

ANSWERS **Same sound, different meaning – Part 2** Questions on page 38.

1 queue   *2* know   *3* wood   *4* Here
5 (*b*)   *6* (*a*)   *7* (*a*)   *8* (*b*)   *9* (*b*)   *10* (*b*)

Telephone directory quiz

1 Write down these names in alphabetical order as if they were in a telephone directory.

Maden Simon T
Mander N. M
Magee P. A
Major Adam S
Madel M. L
March R. F
Major Arthur W
Maden Samuel K

2 Read the following questions. The answer to each one is a telephone number. You will find the numbers in the page from the directory.

Lain D.S, 16 Sunnyview Drive ....**Worton** 51942
Lain K.R, 152 Hayling Road ....**Bucknold** 43668
Lainton Brian G,
   54 Badger Close ....**Grumpton** 4872
Lake Audrey E, 2 New Lane ....**Mapwick** 66001
Lake A.C, 65 King Street ....**Clapton** 77125
Lake Alan K, Brook Farm,
   Stotfold ....**Ickfield** 3174
Laker Dr R.M, Surgery
   (Appointments) ....**Worton** 53675
Laker Dr R.M, 12 Cedar Road ....**Worton** 55812
Lakes Leslie B, 109 Baker Road ......**Bucknold** 44527
Lakes Motors Ltd, Main Road
   Sales and Car Hire ....**Yetford** 80567
   Service and Parts ....**Yetford** 82336
Lakin, J.T, 12 Abbey Walk ....**Ickfield** 3921
Lakin J.T, 39 Crispin Close, ...**Clapton** 70125
Lakin John T, 75 Dunstable Road ....**Grumpton** 4463
Lakin Timber Centres (Ltd),
   Henlow Road ....**Mapwick** 69334
Laking S.A, The Bridge Inn,
   Lawn Lane ....**Ickfield** 3962
Lakins B.N, 9 Dean Close ....**Bucknold** 41429
Lakins P.G, Electrical Contractor,
   29 North Street ....**Clapton** 78342

EXAMPLE: What is the telephone number of Mr Lakins, the electrical contractor?
Answer: Clapton 78342.

What number would you telephone if:
(a) You want to hire a car?
(b) You want to make an appointment to see Dr Laker at his surgery?
(c) Your mother has asked you to ring up her friend, Mrs A. E. Lake?
(d) You want to ring a Mr Lakin. You do not know his initials but you do know he lives in Dunstable Road, Grumpton.
(e) You have heard that Farmer Lake is paying good wages for fruit picking and you want to ring him up to see if he has a job for you?

Turn to page 52 for the answers.

Finding a number in the Yellow Pages

READING When Bill telephones Mr Evans, the shoe repairer, he is told that his boots have not been mended because Mr Evans has been taken ill. He will not be back at work for several weeks. Bill must have his boots repaired before the weekend so he needs a shoe repairer urgently. He looks in his Yellow Pages and finds this:

◆ Shirt Manufacturers
Sartor Ltd, Oldfield Road,
   Clifton . . . .**Mapwick** 61552
Wednesday Shirt Co. Ltd,
   Kingsway Av . . . .**Clapton** 73220

◆ Shoe Repairers
Bootlace Shoe Repairs,
   17 West Street, ...**Worton** 52733
Charlie's High Class Shoe Repairs,
   29 The Arcade . . . .**Yetford** 85469
Instant Repair (Late Closing),
   120 Queensway Walk . . . .**New Town** 63744
North W.K. Ltd, 10 Station Way . . . . .**Bucknold** 45721
   Market Square . . . .**New Town** 55792
   57 Woburn Av . . . .**Clapton** 74176

◆ Shoe Shops
Albright Shoes Ltd, 44 High Street . . .**Grumpton** 4823
Baron Footwear, 15 The Hyde . . . .**Clapton** 72117
Boots and Shoes,
   82 Standbridge Road . . . .**New Town** 66274

WRITING Answer these questions

1 How many shoe repair shops are there?
2 In which town is B. R. Evans, Shoe Repairer? (Look back to page 43.)
3 Bill finishes work at 6 pm. What is the name of the shop Bill would be most likely to choose?
4 What is the telephone number of that shop?
5 Write down two reasons why Bill would choose that shop.

6 Fill in one word for each space. The words you need are in the section shown above.

There are _____ branches of W. K. North Ltd. The telephone number of the Station Way shop is _____ 45721. The shop with the Clapton telephone number is at 57 _____ Avenue. The address of the New Town branch is _____ _____ . Bill did not go to this shoe repairers _____ it closes at 5.30pm.

Turn to page 52 for the answers.

In the Yellow Pages each heading is arranged in alphabetical order so Bill would expect to find Shoe Repairers before Shoe Shops.

Booking a disco by telephone

READING Bill's daughter, Sally, is going to be 18 on Saturday 2 May. The family have hired the hall in the New Town Youth Centre. Sally and her boyfriend have decided to book a disco so they look through the Yellow Pages to see what is available.

◆ Discotheques—Mobile

Bob's Disc Entertainments and Catering,
12 Everton Road . . . .**Ickfield** 3221
Disco King, 71 Barton Road . . . .**Mapwick** 69771
New Town Sound,
16 Linden Walk . . . .**New Town** 24216
Travel Disc, 100 Bradville Street . . . .**Worton** 55721

They decide to ring New Town Sound. Sally dials New Town 24216.

New Town Sound: Hello. New Town 24216. The home of New Town Sound.
Sally: Hello. I'd like to book a disco for Saturday May the Second.
New Town Sound: I'll just check the bookings diary . . . . . Yes, we can manage that date. Where is the disco going to be held?
Sally: It's going to be in the New Town Youth Centre.
New Town Sound: What time do you want us to come?
Sally: My boyfriend suggested 8.30 to midnight.
New Town Sound: That's fine. Can you give me your name, please?
Sally: Yes, I'm Sally Winters. Can you tell me how much it will cost?
New Town Sound: Certainly. We charge £40. That covers lights as well. Is that okay?
Sally: Yes, that's about what we expected.
New Town Sound: Right, Sally. Will you confirm this booking by letter? Just put down the details of day, date, place and time.
Sally: Okay. I'll do that. Goodbye.
New Town Sound: Looking forward to seeing you. 'Bye.

ANSWERS | **Choose the spelling that fits the meaning** Questions on page 39.

1 blue	sale	*6* buy	pears	of
2 your	there	*7* No	queue	
3 for	hour	*8* we'll	week	
4 too	place	*9* I	one	here
5 Would	right	*10* you	would	cheque

ANSWERS | **Picture clues puzzle** Questions on page 39.

1 sale	*2* pairs	*3* son	*4* for
5 here	*6* knows	*7* right	*8* would

Letter writing

Writing a letter of confirmation

Sally decided to write straightaway. Here is a plan of her letter.

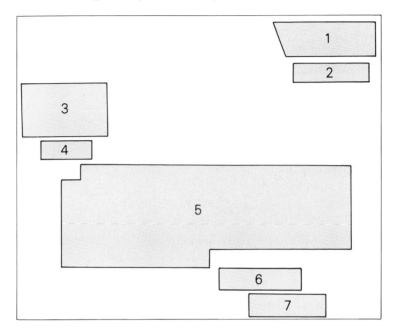

Here are seven shapes which contain the words.

This is one way of setting out a letter. Another layout, which is not indented, is shown in Book 2.

WRITING Match the seven shapes with the seven spaces in the letter plan and write out Sally's letter. Follow exactly the same layout as that given in the letter plan.

Writing a personal letter

Sally wanted her school friend, Julie, to come to her birthday disco, so she wrote to Julie to invite her. Julie lives some distance from New Town and Sally decided to give Julie directions from both the Railway Station and the Bus Station.

WRITING Write Sally's letter to Julie. Use the map on page 33. Follow the same layout as the letter plan, but leave out Box 3. You will have to change Box 4 and Box 5. You will also have to change Box 6 to 'Yours sincerely' because the letter is written to Sally's friend.

Picture story

READING Sally was given some money for her birthday. Read the picture story to see what happened.

Writing a letter of complaint

Sally decided to write to the Manageress of the shop where she had bought the television. There are seven items which Sally needs to put in her letter. They match up with the seven spaces in the letter layout on page 48.

WRITING Write out Sally's letter, using the information given below and the picture story to help you.

Box 1   Sally's address
Box 2   Date
Box 3   Address of shop
Box 4   Dear Madam,
Box 5   Message
Box 6   Ending. Is it 'Yours faithfully' or 'Yours sincerely'?
Box 7   Sally's signature

Have your work marked.

Stamp and envelope crossword

Copy or trace this crossword. Then fill it in.

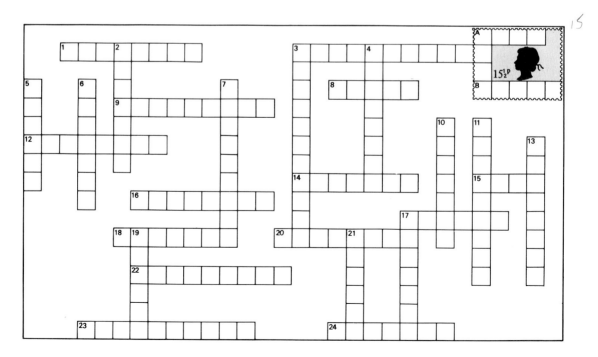

STAMP CLUES

Across
A A summer month that rhymes with soon. (4 letters)
B What is written before "faithfully" or "sincerely" at the end of a letter? (5)

Down
A ULJY is a mixed-up spelling of a summer month. (4)

ENVELOPE CLUES

Across
1 The day you were born. Your _____. (8)
3 A message asking someone to come to a party. (10)
8 Something licked and put on one corner of an envelope. (5)
9 Written after 'Yours' at the end of a personal letter. (9)
12 This month has 29 days once every four years. (8)
14 Your post is put _____ your letterbox. (7)
15 Rearrange *STOP* to make something that arrives through the letter box. (4)
16 The day after Wednesday is _____. (8)
17 The first day back at work most weeks of the year. (6)
18 The month when Sales take place after Christmas. (7)
20 You put a letter inside this. (8)
22 A written statement by the maker of something agreeing to repair or replace it within a certain time if it is faulty. (9)
23 Written after "Yours" at the end of a business letter. (10)
24 A gift given to someone. (7)

Down
2 The day before Wednesday is _____. (7)
3 If you lose your way, you ask for inf_____. (11)
4 We say these words to express gratitude. (5, 3)
5 Something that we use quite often and find helpful we could say is _____. (6)
6 Written on the front of an envelope. (7)
7 The day that is halfway through the week. For some shops it can be a half day closing. (9)
10 I can't read the _____ on this prescription. (7)
11 What you do if you buy something that doesn't work. You write a letter of _____. (9)
13 The first full day of the weekend. (8)
17 Spoken or written information passed from one person to another. (7)
19 The eighth month of the year. (6)
21 You put this inside an envelope. (6)

Turn to page 52 for the solution.

Telephone directory quiz Questions on page 45.

1 Madel M. L
Maden Samuel K
Maden Simon T
Magee P. A
Major Adam S
Major Arthur W
Mander N. M
March R. F

2 (*a*) Yetford 80567
(*b*) Worton 53675
(*c*) Mapwick 66001
(*d*) Grumpton 4463
(*e*) Ickfield 3174

Finding a number in the Yellow Pages Questions on page 46.

1 Six
2 New Town
3 Instant Repair (Late Closing)
4 New Town 63744
5 (a) New Town is his home town.
(b) The shop is open late in the evening.
6 three   Bucknold   Woburn   Market   Square   because

Solution to stamp and envelope crossword on page 50.

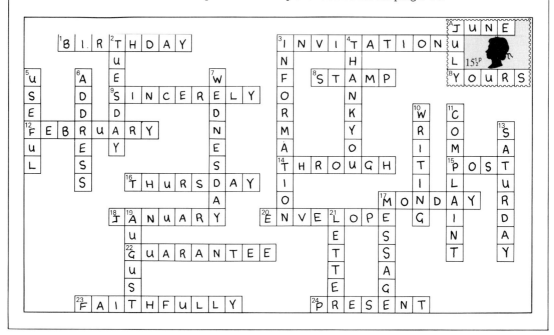

3 Planning a holiday

Home and abroad

READING Read this passage about the tourist who believed he was abroad when really he was still in his own country.

You will see 13 symbols in the passage. Each symbol represents a word.

A story with symbols

Mr Nicholas Scotti lived in San Francisco. In 1977 he planned to fly from America to Italy to visit relatives. On the way, the ✈ made a ⛽ stop at Kennedy Airport, New York. Mr Scotti thought he had arrived at Rome and so he got off the plane.

When he found that his 👪 were not at the ✈Port to meet him, Mr Scotti thought they had been delayed in the heavy traffic of Rome which they had mentioned in their ✉ to him. So he set off to ✎ down their address.

While travelling about New York》, Mr Scotti could not see any of the ancient landmarks which he had expected to find in Rome. He also noticed that many people spoke English with a very strong American accent. However, he just assumed that Americans got everywhere. He also assumed that it was to help them that so many 🛑 were written in English.

Mr Scotti himself spoke very little English and had to ask a 👮 for directions to the 🚌. As luck would have it, the policeman he spoke to was an Italian and so Mr Scotti was given directions in his own language. This, of course, made him absolutely sure that he was really in Rome.

After he had been travelling around in a 🚌 for 12 hours, the driver handed him over to a second policeman. They had an argument, and Mr Scotti said how amazed he was that the Rome police force should employ a man who spoke no Italian.

The police decided to put Mr Scotti on the next aeroplane back to San Francisco He was raced to the airport in a 🚔Police car with sirens screaming.

"See," said Mr Scotti to the interpreter, "I *know* I'm in Italy. That's how they drive there."

WRITING Now write down numbers 1–13 on your paper. Next to number 1 write the word that the first symbol stands for and then complete the list.

Beginnings and endings

WRITING Match the beginnings of these twelve sentences (*LIST A*) with their correct endings from *LIST B*.

LIST A
1 Mr Scotti lived
2 He was going to visit
3 Instead of getting off the aeroplane
4 When his relatives were not there,
5 He was surprised to see
6 Mr Scotti noticed that
7 The first policeman he spoke to
8 Mr Scotti travelled about New York
9 The police decided to
10 They drove to the airport
11 The sirens on the police car
12 Mr Scotti was absolutely sure

LIST B
at full speed.
no ancient landmarks.
were screaming.
everyone could speak English.
his relatives in Rome.
that he was in Italy.
in San Francisco.
he assumed they had been delayed.
was an Italian.
at Rome, he got off at New York.
return Mr Scotti to San Francisco.
by bus.

Turn to page 61 for the answers.

Symbols send messages

Symbols are a way of giving information without using words. They are particularly useful for getting messages across to tourists in foreign countries.

Here are some symbols which tourists who visit this country could find useful.

Write the numbers 1–6 on your paper and next to each number write what the symbol represents.

The answers are on page 63.

Leisure Bay holidays

READING Read this holiday advertisement. Then follow the instructions which are underneath it.

Leisure Bay is the ideal holiday village. You can live in luxury in one of our fully furnished chalets. Many have a **private bath** or a **shower.** All have radio, **TV** and a well equipped kitchen which gives you the freedom to organise your meals when you want them. If you would like an alternative to self-catering, you can enjoy a wide choice of menus in our spacious self-service **restaurant.**

Every chalet is just a few hundred yards from the golden sands of Leisure Bay Beach. Here you can enjoy **swimming, sailing, wind-surfing** or even **water skiing.** Close to the beach is Pleasure Park which offers many forms of recreation including **football, tennis, a putting green** and **horse-riding.** Next to the park is the indoor entertainment centre with a **heated swimming pool,** amusement arcades, and rooms for **snooker, table tennis** and **darts.**

All the bold words could be replaced by signs or symbols.

WRITING Write out the advertisement. Replace as many bold words as you can with symbols.

Symbols save space

READING Symbols save space as well as giving information at a glance. So they are particularly useful in holiday brochures.

Mr and Mrs Stevens are choosing a holiday for themselves and their three children. The youngest child is two-years-old. The six-year-old likes swimming. The eldest child is very keen on horse-riding. They looked through several brochures. They decided against self-catering. Two hotels looked very promising. The prices at both were similar.

Here are the advertisements.

SEAVIEW HOTEL

This popular hotel is situated in a quiet spot on the edge of the town. The beach, Pier and Promenade Shopping Centre are just two Kilometres away.

The hotel has its own heated swimming pool, a sun lounge, a comfortable lounge with colour TV and a licensed bar. Horseriding is available in the neighbouring riding school.

There is a children's play area, a games room and a launderette. Rooms with private bath and toilet are available at an extra charge.

Booking address:
Seaview Hotel, Beachcombe, Pembroke
Tel. 3795

 2 km

SANDY BAY HOTEL

The Sandy Bay Hotel is just a few minutes walk from a safe, sandy beach.

All rooms have wash-basins with hot and cold water. There are two comfortable lounges—one with a colour TV. Special attractions for parents with children include children's menus, nanny service, babysitting and children's play area.

Nearby is an evening entertainment centre with discotheque, ballroom dancing and cabaret.

Booking address:
Sandy Bay Hotel, Coaston, Suffolk
Tel. 54217

   500 m

WRITING

The Stevens family eventually decided to choose the Sandy Bay Hotel.

1 Give at least *THREE* reasons why they preferred the Sandy Bay Hotel to the Seaview Hotel.
2 Write down which hotel you think the eldest child would have preferred, given the choice, and why.
3 Which hotel do you think a family with two teenage children would have preferred? Give reasons for your choice.

Have your work marked.

Organising a holiday

Booking a holiday

READING Mr Stevens telephoned the Sandy Bay Hotel to make a booking. Here are the notes he made on the telephone pad.

> 1 Saturday 8th to Sat 22nd August
> 2 Arrive before 6pm 8th
> 3 Depart before midday 22nd
> 4 1 room with twin beds
> 5 1 room with double bed and cot
> 6 Confirm booking by letter
>   Include deposit of £40

Here is the beginning of his letter confirming the booking.

> 101 Sebastian Road,
> Yardley,
> Worcs.
> 9th March 1983
>
> The Manager,
> Sandy Bay Hotel,
> Coaston,
> Suffolk.
>
> Dear Sir,
>   I am writing to confirm the booking
> of a holiday at your hotel

WRITING Write out the beginning of the letter as it is printed here and then finish the letter. Use the telephone pad notes to help you.

Notice that four of the pad notes are very important and that two others do not need to be mentioned in this letter.

Have your work marked.

Holidays abroad

READING The Stevens family took their holiday in Britain. Many people, for various reasons, go abroad for their holidays.

Here is a holiday postcard sent to the Stevens family from friends who went abroad for a holiday.

July 24th

The weather is hot, a bit too hot. We have to be careful that the children don't get sunstroke! The beach isn't too clean so we use the hotel swimming pool. The food is superb though we have had one or two tummy upsets. One of our suitcases went astray at the airport but we have got it back now.

See you Saturday.
Love, Sue, John and family.

Mr. and Mrs. R. Stevens,

101 Sebastian Road,

Yardley,

WORCS.,

U.K.

WRITING   Answer these questions.

1 Write down two reasons why Sue and John enjoyed the holiday.
  Next, write down three things that weren't so good.
2 Look through a holiday brochure and choose a place and a hotel where you would like to go on holiday. Write down the name of the place and the hotel. Then write down four or five reasons why you would like to go there for a holiday.
3 When you have chosen your holiday, imagine you are there. Write a diary for the most interesting and exciting events of your holiday.

Have your work marked.

Going abroad? What you need to know

READING The Stevens family were so impressed by what their friends had told them that they began to think about going abroad for their next holiday. There was one small problem. They did not know how to begin to arrange a holiday abroad.

The next day, Mrs Stevens came home from work smiling. A friend had lent her a very useful booklet which was called *Going Abroad? What You Need to Know.* As she read through this with her husband, they underlined the words which they wanted to know more about.

CHOOSING A HOLIDAY
Think about 1) Where do you want to go? 2) What do you want to do? 3) Where do you want to stay? (Hotel, Holiday Camp, etc.) 4) How do you want to travel? When you have some answers to these questions, go to a Travel Agency and ask the travel agent for some holiday brochures and for some advice.

BOOKING A HOLIDAY
When you have decided where you want to go, take the brochure to the travel agent and fill in the booking form. When you book the holiday you will have to pay a deposit. Don't forget to ask for a receipt. The travel agent will tell you when you will have to pay the balance. Read the booking conditions carefully.

APPLYING FOR A PASSPORT
There are two types of passport.
1 A British Visitor's Passport. This is only valid for 12 months. This passport can only be used in certain countries. It can be obtained over the counter at some post offices.
2 A United Kingdom Passport. This is valid for 10 years and is normally valid for all countries. Allow 4 weeks for delivery. Application forms can be found in main post offices. A husband, wife and children under 16 can all be included on one passport.

APPLYING FOR FOREIGN CURRENCY
About two weeks before you go on holiday, go to a Bank and apply for the foreign currency you will need on holiday. You can take spending money in the form of travellers cheques. The Bank will explain how to use these.

Match the word with the meaning

WRITING *LIST A* contains words from the booklet. Write down each one, then write the correct definition from *LIST B*. The definitions are in the wrong order. You may use a dictionary.

LIST A
1 Travel Agency
2 brochure
3 booking form
4 deposit
5 receipt
6 balance
7 booking conditions
8 passport
9 valid
10 currency

LIST B
A The type of money in use in a country.
B A small booklet or document which says who a person is. It is taken when travelling abroad.
C A booklet which gives information about something. For example, a holiday brochure.
D A business that arranges journeys and holiday bookings.
E A payment of part of the cost of something. For example, a holiday.
F A set of agreements a traveller accepts when making a booking for a holiday.
G The sum of money which is still owed for something after the deposit has been paid.
H A form which you fill in to book a holiday or a hotel.
I Written or printed proof that a payment has been received.
J Can be used legally.

Turn to page 63 for the answers.

ANSWERS **Beginnings and endings** Questions on page 55.

1 Mr Scotti lived in San Francisco.
2 He was going to visit his relatives in Rome.
3 Instead of getting off the aeroplane at Rome, he got off at New York.
4 When his relatives were not there, he assumed they had been delayed.
5 He was surprised to see no ancient landmarks.
6 Mr Scotti noticed that everyone could speak English.
7 The first policeman he spoke to was an Italian.
8 Mr Scotti travelled about New York by bus.
9 The police decided to return Mr Scotti to San Francisco.
10 They drove to the airport at full speed.
11 The sirens on the police car were screaming.
12 Mr Scotti was absolutely sure that he was in Italy.

Applying for a British Visitor's Passport

READING Here is part of the application form for a British Visitor's Passport. Mr Stevens has filled it in himself.

		FILE NUMBER
Form VP	**APPLICATION FOR BRITISH VISITOR'S PASSPORT (FOR PERSON WHO MUST BE AGED 8 OR OVER)**	**SPECIMEN**

VALID FOR CERTAIN COUNTRIES ONLY (See Section 8)
FEE £5.50 DOCUMENTS REQUIRED (See Note (viii))
TO BE COMPLETED IN INK (PREFERABLY BY BALL POINT PEN) BY THE APPLICANT (FOR A CHILD UNDER SIXTEEN THIS SHOULD BE A PARENT) AFTER FIRST CAREFULLY READING THE NOTES ON PAGES 3 AND 4.

FOR OFFICIAL USE ONLY

Passport Number

Date of Issue

1 PERSON FOR WHOM PASSPORT IS REQUIRED

Height ① 5 ft 11 ins	Private address in the United Kingdom, Isle of Man or Channel Islands. (IN BLOCK CAPITALS) ② 101 SEBASTIAN ROAD, YARDLEY, WORCS,	SURNAME (IN BLOCK CAPITALS) State whether Mr., Mrs., Miss or Ms. ③ MR. STEVENS
Height (See Note (vi)). ....metres	Postcode WPI 2WO	Forenames in full (IN BLOCK CAPITALS) ④ ROGER PAUL
	Maiden Surname (IN BLOCK CAPITALS) if applicant is a woman who is or has been married	Date of Birth 21st JUNE 1950 Age ⑤
Visible distinguishing marks NONE ⑥		Town of Birth ⑦	Country of Birth BRITAIN

2 PARTICULARS OF WIFE/HUSBAND (if to be included in the same Visitor's Passport) (See Note (v) (a))

Height ......ft .....ins	Forenames and Surname in full (IN BLOCK CAPITALS)		Date of Birth
Height (See Note (vi)). ....metres	Maiden Surname (IN BLOCK CAPITALS)	Town of Birth	Country of Birth
Visible distinguishing marks			

3 PARTICULARS OF CHILDREN, UNDER 16, IF TO BE INCLUDED IN PASSPORT

(including adopted or step children).   Note:–Section 4 must also be completed and signed.

Forenames (in full)	Surname	Date of Birth	Sex	Relationship to Applicant
CHRISTOPHER MARK		30th JULY 1973	MALE	SON
ANDREA CLARE		19th APRIL 1978	FEMALE	DAUGHTER
PHILIP JOHN		1st MAY 1979	MALE	SON

4 PARENT'S CONSENT FOR PERSON UNDER 18   (see Note (v) (e) on Page 3)

I (full names) ...ROGER PAUL STEVENS.............of (address) 101 SEBASTIAN ROAD YARDLEY WORCS. ....being the (relationship) ....FATHER........................... of (name(s) ...CHRISTOPHER, ANDREA and PHILIP................hereby request that he/she/they* be granted the facilities here applied for. I declare that my rights in respect of the child/children* have not been limited in any way by the order of any court having jurisdiction over him/her/them* ⑧

*Delete as appropriate   Signature ...Roger P. Stevens............................

5 SIGNATURE OF CHILD UNDER 16 WHERE PASSPORT IS FOR HIM/HER (See Note (v) (f))

Understanding a passport application form

1 In box 1 Mr Stevens has written his height. What is it? He also has to give his height in metres. Look at this table and write down his height in metres.

Ft. Ins.		Metres	Ft. Ins.		Metres	Ft. Ins.		Metres
4	10	1.47	5	3	1.60	5	8	1.73
4	11	1.50	5	4	1.63	5	9	1.75
5	0	1.52	5	5	1.65	5	10	1.78
5	1	1.55	5	6	1.68	5	11	1.80
5	2	1.57	5	7	1.70	6	0	1.83

2 A postcode is: A group of letters and numbers that means a particular area. What is Mr Stevens' postcode?

3 Mr Stevens' title is Mr. You know what Mrs and Miss mean. What does Ms mean?

4 What is another word for Forenames?

5 Look at Mr Stevens' date of birth. Write down his age.

6 Visible distinguishing marks are things like scars on a person's hands or face. Mr Stevens has a scar on his stomach. Why did he not mention this on the form?

7 Mr Stevens was born in the town where he now lives. What is the town?

8 At the bottom of the form "*Delete as appropriate" means cross out the words which are not needed. Which words will Mr Stevens cross out?

(*a*) he/she/they   (*b*) child/children   (*c*) him/her/them

The answers are on page 67.

ANSWERS **Symbols send messages** Questions on page 55.

1 Camping and Caravan Site 300 metres
2 Parking
3 Ladies' Toilet
4 Service Station
5 Gents' Toilet
6 Tourist Information

ANSWERS **Match the word with the meaning** Questions on page 61.

1 D   *2 C*   *3 H*   *4 E*   *5 I*   *6 G*   *7 F*   *8 B*   *9 J*   *10 A*

Filling in an application form

WRITING Write the number of each box on the top section of the passport form (1–8) Make sure you leave a few lines for box 2. Next to each box number write down the information which would be in the box if you were filling in a passport form for yourself.

Do not fill in the other sections of the form.

Have your work marked.

Holiday competition

While the Stevens family were deciding where to go for their holiday abroad, they received this holiday competition form. The prize was a fortnight's holiday for a whole family in the Bahamas with all expenses paid and free car hire.

See if you can work out the answers. Write them on your paper.

WIN THE HOLIDAY OF A LIFETIME
COMPETITION ENTRY FORM

Part one
Rearrange the letters of the words in this list to spell the names of ten European countries where you can enjoy an exciting holiday. To help you, we have printed the currency of the country next to each jumbled name.

?	CURRENCY	NAME OF THE COUNTRY
CERFAN	franc	1
YALTI	lira	2
NIPSA	peseta	3
ECEGRE	drachma	4
ZWELTSANDRI	franc	5
LAGUTROP	escudo	6
TRIASUA	schilling	7
STEW MARGENY	deutschmark	8
THENRENLADS	guilder	9
NEDKRAM	krone	10

Turn to page 71 for the answers.

Part two

Can you organise a holiday? Here are 12 things you should do to organise your holiday well. All you have to do is write them down in the most sensible order.

1 Arrange for pets to be looked after.
2 Lock up carefully.
3 Check tickets and travel documents.
4 Book holiday.
5 Turn off water and gas.
6 Get passport.
7 Tell neighbours you are going away.
8 Book taxi.
9 Do holiday shopping.
10 Cancel papers and milk.
11 Order foreign currency from a Bank.
12 Pack cases.

Part three

Here are the first four lines of a limerick – a short poem in five lines. Write out the last line. Make sure it rhymes with the last word of the first two lines.

A brave family sets off in June
On a holiday flight to the moon.
But they found it a bore
Without a sea shore

_ _ _ _ _ _ _ _ _ _ _ _ _ _ _

Now fill in this part of the form. Then take the whole competition entry form to any Travel Agency before midnight on April 1st.

SURNAME Mr/Mrs/Miss/Ms* _ _ _ _ _ _ _ _ _ _ _ _ _ _

FORENAMES _

HOME ADDRESS _ _ _ _ _ _ _ _ _ _ _ _ _ _ _ _ _ _

 _ _ _ _ _ _ _ _ _ _ _ _ _ _ _ _ _

 _ _ _ _ _ _ _ _ _ _ _ _ _ _ _ _ _

TELEPHONE NUMBER _ _ _ _ _ _ _ _ _ _ _

*Delete as appropriate

NOTE: 'Surname' means last name, eg Stevens.
'Forenames' means first names, eg Kevin James.

Have your work marked.

On holiday

Mystery holiday photographs

While Mr Stevens was on holiday, he saw something coming up out of the water towards him. He quickly took these photographs.

DISCUSSION Discuss these questions.

1 What was coming out of the water?
2 What was it doing there?
3 What happened next?

WRITING Write a story called "Underwater mystery" – or give the story your own title.

Have your work marked.

ANSWERS **Understanding a passport application form** Questions on page 63.

1 1.8 metres
2 WP1 2WO
3 Ms is a title for a woman who does not wish to call herself either Mrs or Miss.
4 First names or Christian names
5 In 1983 – 33 years old.
6 Because a scar on his stomach would not be visible.
7 Yardley
8 The words crossed out are:
   (a) he/she   (b) child   (c) him/her

The Stevens family abroad

READING The Stevens family decided to go to the Hotel Continental in Spain. They chose this hotel because they liked the picture in the brochure and because they thought the hotel could provide all they wanted. By the end of the holiday, several things had disappointed them. This is what Mr and Mrs Stevens told their friends:

Report 1 "Although the beds in our rooms were very comfortable, we did not have the view over the bay which we had seen in the brochure. There was a lot for the children to do. The hotel had a children's play area, a games room and a swimming pool. There was also a sleep patrol to keep an eye on the children at night while we relaxed in one of the hotel lounges or strolled along the fascinating streets. The disco was a bit loud for us and even woke up the children once or twice. We all liked the food but we did have a few tummy upsets. It was a pity that there were no special menus for children. We thought we would have a private bathroom but found that we had to share one. Thank goodness the hotel provided towels."

Paul and Clare, a honeymoon couple, had a different opinion:

Report 2 "The first thing we noticed when we arrived was the heated swimming pool. It was fabulous. We enjoyed sitting beside it on the sun terrace after a swim, sipping cool drinks served by friendly waiters. The food in the restaurant was very good, but we would have liked a wider choice of menus. The hotel organised interesting coach tours but we preferred playing tennis or wind surfing. The beach is only a short walk from the hotel. The late night disco was superb. We danced till two in the morning."

Writing a hotel report

WRITING Write your own hotel report on the Hotel Continental using the information given in reports 1 and 2. Do not use the names of the people. Use these headings to help you.

1 SITUATION (Is the hotel in an attractive or pleasant area?)
2 ACCOMMODATION (Are the rooms comfortable? Is there a bathroom?)
3 FOOD (How good is the food? Is there a choice? Is the service reasonable?)
4 SPORT AND LEISURE (What does the hotel provide?)
5 WHAT SORT OF PERSON WOULD LIKE THIS HOTEL?

Have your work marked.

Surprise Adventure Holidays

Parts: Mark
　　　Dad
　　　Mum
　　　Lynne
　　　Slave driver
　　　Man in uniform
　　　Manager
　　　Fred

Scene: On board a Viking galley. The holiday-makers are rowing, watched over by a huge, bearded man.

Mark:	It's hard work this rowing, isn't it, Dad?
Dad:	Ah, that is only because you're not used to it.
Mum:	You'd think they would have told us that we had to row our own galley.
Lynne:	Yes. I imagined there would be handsome, brawny crewmen to do that for us.
Mark:	While we sipped cool drinks on sun loungers.
Dad:	Well if they had warned us, it wouldn't have been a Surprise Adventure Holiday, would it?
Mum:	You mean like it said in the brochure?
Dad:	Of course.
Mum:	Oh, you're so clever, Dad. You've always got an answer.
Lynne:	Was that near-collision with the car ferry another one of the surprises?
Dad:	It could have been.
Lynne:	That was so exciting. Everybody rowed for all they were worth.
Mark:	Yes. Even that woman in the fur coat.
Mum:	(*Jealously*) I can't think why she chose to wear a fur. It is summer.
Dad:	Perhaps she thought it would be chilly on a boat like this.
Slave driver:	(*Cracking whip*) Do you mind. That is my pet gorilla you're talking about.
Mum:	Pet gorilla? Why ever did you want to bring a gorilla on a trip like this?
Slave driver:	Because he's the one who rows this galley back when you lot get off.
Lynne:	How do we get back then?

Slave driver: That's another one of the surprises. But we do provide a return journey do-it-yourself kit.

Mum: (*Bursting into tears*) I told you it was never wise to book a holiday at the undertakers.

Dad: Don't start that again. He told me that lots of his clients had been on this adventure holiday.

Mark: I wonder where they all are now?

Lynne: Hey, look! This boat's just sprung a leak. We'll have to swim for it.

Slave driver: Just stick your finger in it. We'll be at the landing jetty in a minute.

Mum: What are those logs floating on the surface?

Slave driver: Those logs are crocodiles.

Dad: Where have they come from?

Mark: I've never heard of crocodiles in the North Sea.

Slave driver: They are the Adventure Island security guards. Don't slip on your way off the boat.

When all the passengers have left the boat, they are told to queue at the taxi sign.

Lynne: Good job we got here first.

Mark: Yes, I'm exhausted.

Mum: I hope the taxi driver goes slowly. I feel a bit seasick.

Dad: Ah, here's somebody.

Man in uniform: Right then. Who's first for the taxi?

Dad: We are.

Man in Uniform: Right. Put your cases in here then.

Mum: In where?

Man in uniform: In this wheelbarrow.

Mark: But where's the taxi?

Man in uniform: This is it.

Lynne: What, that wheelbarrow?

Man in uniform: Yes. And hurry up and bring it back or it will take all day to shift this lot.

Dad: This is ridiculous.

Mum: Perhaps it's another one of those surprises, Dad.

Dad: Oh, Come on then.

Later, at the camp reception desk.

Manager: Welcome to Adventure Island. I hope you enjoy your stay.

Mum: Where is our log cabin?

Manager: Wherever you like, madam.

Dad: You mean we have a choice?

Manager: Certainly, sir. You can build it wherever you like. The saws and nails are in the building marked "Survival Workshop".

Lynne: You mean we have to build it ourselves?

Manager: Just another of the little surprises we offer here to make sure our guests have a really enjoyable holiday.

Mark: Where is the best place to build?

Manager: I'm glad you mentioned that. Here's a map of the island. Just avoid the places marked with a black cross.

Mum: But the whole island is nearly covered with black crosses.

Manager: There are one or two nice places where you will be well away from the snake-infested swamp and the four acres of quicksand.

Dad: What, no anacondas?

Manager: Oh yes, sir. They live in the adventure swimming pool. We used to keep the piranha fish in there, but the poison springs killed them off.

Lynne: Couldn't we just stay in that hut over there?

Manager: Certainly not. That belongs to the Survival Superintendent. Hey, Fred!

Fred: (*Coming out of shed*) Yes. What do you want?

Manager: Can you explain about the do-it-yourself return journey kit?

Fred: Sure. At the end of your holiday, you come back here and give me the green voucher.

Mark: You mean the one with a skull and crossbones on it?

Mum: I thought that was just a joke.

Fred: Oh no, madam. You can't get home without it unless you can swim in a suit of armour.

Dad: Why a suit of armour?

Fred: Because we don't feed the security crocodiles during the holiday season.

Dad: Oh.

Lynne: Can we have the kit now?

Fred: Yes. But open it carefully.

Mark: Why?

Fred: Because some of them are booby-trapped.

Manager: It's all part of the fun.

ANSWERS **Competition entry form Part one** Questions on page 64.

1 FRANCE	6 PORTUGAL
2 ITALY	7 AUSTRIA
3 SPAIN	8 WEST GERMANY
4 GREECE	9 NETHERLANDS
5 SWITZERLAND	10 DENMARK

Adventure Island

Two days later the family decide to escape. They open the do-it-yourself return journey kit carefully and find these items:

3 extra-long stilts
1 crocodile harness
1 pair of water skis
50 kilos of fire lighters
1 asbestos suit
1 book called *How to write your own Will*
2 oil drums
1 tube of super glue

1 ball of string
15 metres of rope
1 packet of large balloons
Pirates' disguise kit, complete with wooden leg
4 tyre inner tubes
1 roll of polythene sheeting
1 parachute

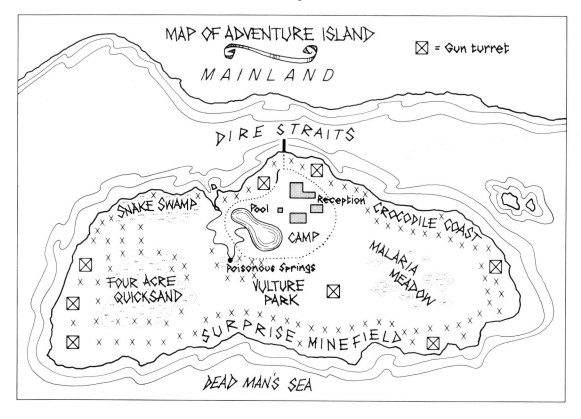

MAP OF ADVENTURE ISLAND

☒ = Gun turret

MAINLAND

DIRE STRAITS

SNAKE SWAMP

Pool

Reception

CROCODILE COAST

CAMP

Poisonous Springs

FOUR ACRE QUICKSAND

VULTURE PARK

MALARIA MEADOW

SURPRISE MINEFIELD

DEAD MAN'S SEA

DISCUSSION Look carefully at the map of Adventure Island.

1 Which would be the best place for the family to escape from?
2 How many different ways could they escape using the do-it yourself kit?

WRITING Now write down how they escaped EITHER as a play OR as a story.

4 Invention and communication

The telephone

Radio-phone

Look at this picture carefully.

WRITING Answer each of these questions in as much detail as you can.

1 What is unusual about the briefcase on the bench?
2 What does the man seem to be doing? Look at his face. What clue does this give you?
3 The briefcase is a kind of telephone. How does it work, do you think?
4 What sort of people would be likely to use a telephone like this?
5 What are the advantages and disadvantages of having a telephone that can be carried about like this one?

The story behind the picture

Imagine that you are the inventor of the briefcase phone. Write down the story of your invention from the moment you first had the idea up to the time you were using the telephone on the park bench as shown in the photograph.

1 Begin your story by saying when you had the idea. Say what day and what date it was. Say where you were and what you were looking at. Then explain what gave you the idea.
2 Say why you chose to make the telephone fit into a briefcase. What are the advantages of this design?
3 Explain (a) how the telephone works
         (b) where it can be used
         (c) how someone knows he or she is being called on the briefcase phone.
4 Explain why you were using the briefcase phone in the park.
5 Say who you think will buy your briefcase phone and what the phone will cost.

Two inventors of the telephone

READING In April 1980 a new radio-phone, which fits into a briefcase, was shown at an exhibition on communications. This radio-phone has been specially designed for the business person who has to travel from place to place. He or she will find it a useful aid because it will work in cars, on trains, on ferries or almost anywhere. If someone is calling the person on his or her radio-phone, instead of a bell ringing, a red light on the briefcase flashes on and off.

Before the radio-phone was invented business people were afraid that they would miss urgent phone calls or an important letter while they were away from the office. Now that they can carry their own phone with them, this fear has been brought to an end. They can speak to their secretary, or to anyone, from wherever they are, even from a park bench!

The inventor of this radio-phone is Mr Graham Thomas. He put his invention through a number of tests to make sure it worked properly. He now hopes to sell 500 radio-phones a year for £1,000 each. Until recently it was against the law to have a telephone that was not supplied and installed by the Post Office. This rule was changed in October 1979, making the radio-phone entirely legal.

Alexander Graham Bell invented a very different-looking telephone over a century ago. It was first shown to the public at an exhibition in the USA in 1876. Bell was a teacher of speech to deaf people, and he had been trying to invent a machine that would help them. This machine, in its modern form, is now the telephone which is used in millions of homes all over the world.

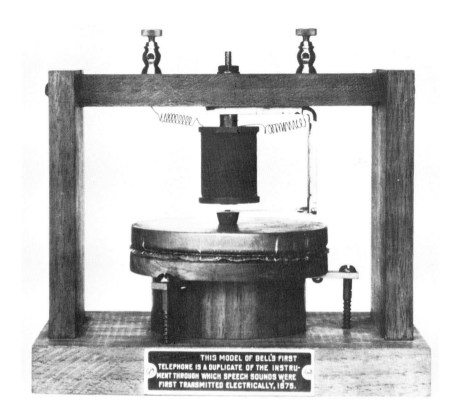

THIS MODEL OF BELL'S FIRST
TELEPHONE IS A DUPLICATE OF THE INSTRU-
MENT THROUGH WHICH SPEECH SOUNDS WERE
FIRST TRANSMITTED ELECTRICALLY, 1875.

Word and sentence matching

In the story "Two inventors of the telephone", ten words have been underlined.

WRITING Write them on your paper. Use your dictionary to find out the meaning of any word you do not know.

Now write out these ten sentences. Begin each sentence on a new line. Fill in each space with the right word from your list of ten words.

1 If something is _____ then it is allowed by law.
2 _____ is a word which means help.
3 A person who makes up or produces something new is an _____.
4 _____ means that something has been set up and is ready for use.
5 An _____ is a show of objects to which people may go.
6 A period of 100 years is a _____.
7 Something which is very important and must be dealt with quickly is _____.
8 _____ means ways of sending information between two places.
9 Being afraid of a thing is the same thing as having _____.
10 An inventor's work is his _____.

Turn to page 78 for the answers.

Telephone crossword

Read the story "Two inventors of the telephone" again. Make a copy of this crossword on your paper. Then fill in the answers.

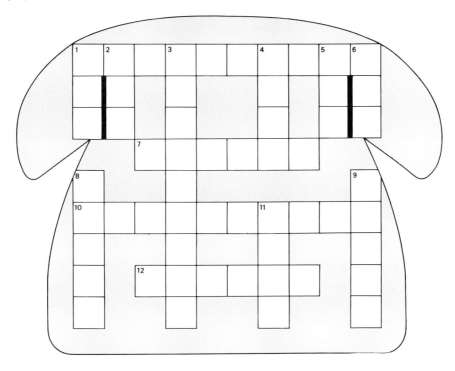

Across
 1 The name of the new invention. (10)
 7 Something a business person may miss while away from the office. (6)
 10 An organisation which supplies and installs telephones. (4, 6)
 12 A forename shared by both inventors. (6)

Down
 1 The colour of the flashing light on the briefcase. (3)
 2 This invention is a great help or a useful _____ (3) to the business person.
 3 People who make things like the telephone are called this. (9)
 4 A place where you would normally find a modern telephone. (4)
 5 Recently made. Opposite of old. (3)
 6 This invention has brought the fear of every businessman to an _____. (3)
 8 From even a park bench someone can _____ to their secretary. (5)
 9 This invention has been through a number of these to prove it works. (5)
 11 Another word for the worry of every business person. (4)

Turn to page 84 for the solution.

A perfect match

WRITING Write out on five separate lines the words printed in column *A*. You now have the beginnings of five separate sentences. Write out the rest of each sentence by choosing the right words from columns *B* and *C*.

A	*B*	*C*
The man	radio-phone set	thoroughly for 18 months.
Before the invention was demonstrated	of the telephone	is making a phone call.
Each	a red light flashes	have the same Christian name.
When you are being called	who is sitting on the bench	costs £1,000.
Both the inventors	it was tested	on your briefcase.

When you have finished, read the sentences to your friend to make sure that they make sense.

Beginnings and endings

Here are the beginnings of five sentences. Read them carefully then finish each sentence so that it makes sense.

1 Mr Graham Thomas has invented . . . .
2 I saw the new invention at . . . .
3 The radio-phone is useful for business people because . . . .
4 To make sure the radio-phone worked properly . . . .
5 In 1876, in the USA, ...

Here are the endings of five sentences. Make up the beginnings. When you have finished all ten sentences, read them to someone to make sure they make sense.

1 . . . . for business people who travel from place to place.
2 . . . . instead of a bell ringing.
3 . . . . for £1,000 each.
4 . . . . was invented by Alexander Graham Bell.
5 . . . . installed by the Post Office.

ANSWERS **Word and sentence matching** Questions on page 76.

1 legal	*2* aid	*3* inventor	*4* installed	*5* exhibition
6 century	*7* urgent	*8* communications	*9* fear	*10* invention

---

Could you be an inventor?

READING Read this true story about Mrs Betty Graham. It shows how a very simple invention could make you a fortune.

A fortune in error

A former office secretary who made a fortune by inventing the white fluid used by typists to erase mistakes has died in Dallas, Texas.

Mrs Betty Graham, 56, had the idea in the 1950s, when she was trying to support herself and her son, Michael Nesmith.

He was also destined for world-wide recognition as a singer with "The Monkees" pop group. He is now a country rock guitarist.

But in 1951, as secretary to the chairman of the board at a Dallas bank, Mrs Graham was barely able to make ends meet.

She worked at night as a freelance artist, and noted that artists never corrected by erasing, but always painted over errors.

She founded the Liquid Paper Corporation to market the fluid, which is applied with a brush to blot out letters. Last November she sold her stock to the Gillette Company for $47,500,000.

Definitions you might need before you talk about this story:

error	mistake
fluid	a liquid
erase	to rub out
destined	intended to be in the future
recognition	being recognised or noticed
freelance	person working for himself or herself and not for an employer
market	to offer for sale
to make ends meet	to be able to live off what you earn

Think and talk

DISCUSSION
1 Why did Mrs Betty Graham have two jobs?
2 How did watching artists correcting their mistakes give her the idea for her invention of "Liquid Paper"?
3 Was she clever, observant or just lucky?
4 Who could have been the first few people she shared this idea with?
5 When Mrs Graham died, she was a very rich woman. If you had that much money, what would you do with it?

An invention of your own

Can you think of an invention that:
- (a) would be useful
- (b) would save time
- (c) would save work
- (d) would be bought by many people?

NOTE: Many so-called "inventions" are improvements of earlier inventions. Your invention could be either a brand new idea or an improvement of an existing machine or product.

Here are some ideas to help you.
1 Invent a new way of using a lawn mower so that you can cut the grass while sitting in your armchair in the lounge.
2 Think of an invention to help people keep their spectacles clear while they are out walking on a rainy day.
3 Design a multi-purpose backscratcher suitable for people who differ in age, height and size.
4 Invent one or two new ways of using a small bulb or torch as part of another product so that that product can be used in the dark.

Fill in a form

Once you have invented something, you need to register it so that nobody can steal your idea. In the United Kingdom you would write to The Patent Office, 25 Southampton Buildings, London WC 2A 1AY.

For the purpose of this book we have made up a company called The New Invention Company Limited. Imagine that you are writing to this company to register your invention. Copy out this form and fill in your own details.

Write a letter

WRITING You have heard of a company who might be interested in making and marketing your invention. Write a letter to the Managing Director of the firm (make up a suitable one).

In the first part of the letter, write down in clear sentences the information which you put down for numbers 6–11 on your application form to The New Invention Company. In the second part of your letter, explain why your invention would sell well.

Look back to page 48 if you need help with laying out a letter.

THE NEW INVENTION COMPANY LIMITED

Application for registration of an invention

(PLEASE WRITE IN BLOCK CAPITALS)

1   NAME OF APPLICANT...

2   DATE OF BIRTH..

3   COUNTRY OF BIRTH...

4   ADDRESS...

     ....

5   TELEPHONE NUMBER.........................

6   NAME OF INVENTION.......................................

7   SIZE.......................................

8   WEIGHT......................................

9   COLOUR......................................

10   MADE OF..

11   WHAT IT DOES, HOW IT WORKS AND HOW IT IS POWERED................

     ....

     ....

     ....

     ....

12   DRAW A CLEAR, LABELLED DIAGRAM OF YOUR INVENTION ON THE BACK OF

     THIS FORM.

Signature.............................Date........................

The telephone in use

Words and pictures

WRITING On the *LEFT* are six captions (groups of words). On the *RIGHT* are six pictures, one for each caption. Decide which is the most sensible order for the captions. Then write them out carefully, putting each one on a separate line.

When you have done that, match each caption with the right picture.

EXAMPLE: If you think caption *1* is matched with picture *C,* write out caption *1* and write Picture *C* after it.

CAPTIONS   *PICTURES*

1 You think of looking for the telephone numbers of camera   *A*
shops in the Yellow Pages.

2 You see a camera advertised.   *B*
You want to buy it.

3 So you turn to "Photographic Equipment and   *C*
Supplies – Retailers" in the Yellow Pages.

4 When you telephone each shop you write down the name of *D*
the shop, the price of the camera and the phone number (in
case you want to phone again).

5 You wonder which camera shop in your area sells the   *E*
camera (which you have seen advertised) at the cheapest
price.

6 You find *CAMERA* in the Yellow Pages but it says: *F*
SEE PHOTOGRAPHIC EQUIPMENT AND SUPPLIES –
RETAILERS

Turn to page 84 for the answers.

82

Choose the right word

READING Jo is telephoning a local camera shop. She wants to find out if it sells a camera which has been advertised on television.

Some words have been left out of this conversation. Where you see _____ choose one word which fits into the sentence and makes sense. If you have any difficulty, read what is said before the _____ and then read on a little bit.

Number from 1 to 52 on your paper. Do not write in this book.

Jo:	Hello.	
Camera Craft:	Hello Camera Craft.	
Jo:	Do ____ have a *K*100 Electro Flash with built-in electronic flash	1
	and telephoto lens in stock? It was ___ on television last ____ and	2 3
	I would like to ____ one.	4
Camera C:	As far as I know, those ____ are not available in this area yet.	5
Jo:	What can I do to find out where they are on sale?	
Camera C:	You could ring Tele Data.	
Jo:	Is that a ____ shop?	6
Camera C:	Oh no. Tele Data is an information service.	
Jo:	Can you tell me the ____ please?	7
Camera C:	Yes. It is 01 200 0200.	
Jo:	____ you. Goodbye.	8
Camera C:	____	9

Jo dials the number for Tele Data

Tele Data:	Hello. ____ Data.	10
Jo:	Hello. I would like to ____ where I can ____ a type of camera	11 12
	which I saw advertised on ____ last night.	13
Tele Data:	Can you tell me what ____ of camera it is?	14
Jo:	Yes, it is a *K*100 Electro Flash with ____ electronic flash and ___	15 16
	lens. I have already rung one camera shop in this area.	
Tele Data:	What did the shop assistant tell you?	
Jo:	He said that type of ____ was not ____ in this area yet. He then	17 18
	told me to ____ you.	19
Tele Data:	Which town are you ringing from?	
Jo:	From New Town.	
Tele Data:	Well, the nearest large camera ____ to you is at Hunts Cross.	20
Jo:	That is about seven ____ from ____ . Are they selling the *K*100?	21 22
Tele Data:	The Tele Data service provides ____ on shops and services	23
	It cannot say what is in stock in each ____ . I can give you the	24
	number of the ____ shop in Hunts Cross. You could telephone	25
	them and ____ them if they have ____ in stock.	26 27
Jo:	That is a good ____ .	28

Tele Data: The name of the shop is Camera Discount and the number is Hunts Cross 21753.

Jo: Thank you. Bye.

Jo dials the number for Camera Discount

Discount: ____ . Camera Discount. Can I ____ you?	29 30
Jo: Yes. Do you have a *K100* ____ with built-in ____ flash and	31 32
telephoto ____ ?	33
Discount: Yes. They have just ____ .	34
Jo: Oh, wonderful, I would ____ to buy one, but I can't come over	35
to your shop ____ Thursday. Do you think you will	36
have ____ out by then?	37
Discount: They are very popular but I could reserve ____ for you though.	38
Jo: Would you, please? I really do ____ to buy one.	39
Discount: Certainly. Would you ____ me your name and address?	40
Jo: Yes. (*Fill in your name and address ____*)	41
Discount: That's fine.	
Jo: Oh, by the way, what time do you close on a ____ ?	42
Discount: We are open until 6 o'clock.	
Jo: Oh, is the shop near a car ____ ?	43
Discount: Yes. Just follow the signs marked "Town ____ " and you will see	44
a multi-storey ____ park. When you have parked the car, come	45
back to the entrance, ____ the road and you will see this ____ .	46 47
Jo: Thank you. There is just one last thing. I ____ to ask you the price.	48
Discount: It is ____ offer at the moment for £39·95.	49
Jo: That's even better than I ____ Thank you. Bye.	50
Discount: Bye. We'll ____ you on ____	51 52

Check your answers on page 89.

ANSWERS **Crossword** on page 77.

Across: 1 Radio-phone 7 Letter 10 Post Office 12 Graham
Down: 1 Red 2 Aid 3 Inventors 4 Home 5 New
6 End 8 Speak 9 Tests 11 Fear

ANSWERS **Words and pictures** Questions on page 82.

(Captions and pictures)
2D 5A 1F 6B 3E 4C

The portable Payphone

READING Payphones can be seen in clubs, hotels, shops, blocks of flats, community centres, garages, factories, hospitals and in many other places. They are usually firmly fixed to a wall.

Here is a picture of a portable Payphone.

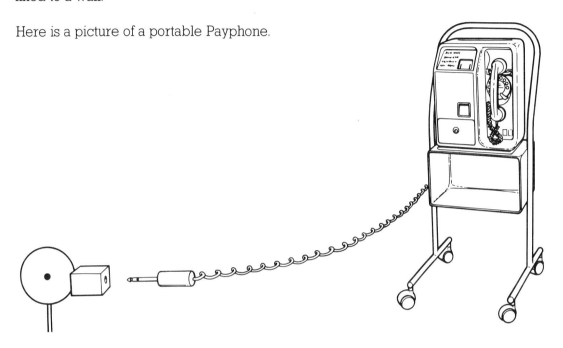

Every Payphone has a carrying handle and a bracket for storing a long telephone cord. The Payphone is connected to the exchange line by plug and socket. The cord between the Payphone and the plug is about 7.6 metres long. A separate bell is provided near the socket so that you know that someone is trying to ring you when the Payphone is unplugged.

How to use the Payphone

WRITING Here are the four instructions for using the Payphone. They are printed here in the wrong order. Write them out in the right order. Put each instruction on a new line.

1 When you hear rapid pips press in a coin.
2 Lift receiver and listen for continuous purring.
3 To continue a dialled call put in more money during conversation or when you hear rapid pips again.
4 Dial number or code and number.

Turn to page 87 for the answers.

Three reasons for having a Payphone

1 A Payphone gives a controlled telephone service which is useful for customer, staff or client.
2 The more use people make of the Payphone, the more rebate the renter gets.
3 The Payphone is suitable for multi-tenancy buildings or blocks of flats and most other areas to which the public have access.

| WRITING | Match the eight words in *LIST A* with the eight definitions in *LIST B*. First write down the word then write the correct definition after it.

LIST A
1 controlled
2 customer
3 staff
4 client
5 rebate
6 renter
7 multi-tenancy buildings
8 access

LIST B
A a person who buys something from a shop.
B an official paying back of part of a payment.
C a regulated use of something.
D being able to enter a place or having the right to enter a place.
E the group of workers who do the work of an organisation.
F large buildings which are rented by more than one tenant or organisation.
G a person who pays someone, for example a lawyer, to do a job or piece of work for him.
H a person who pays money to rent something.

Turn to page 93 for the answers.

A Payphone for the Community Centre

Here is a plan of a Community Centre.

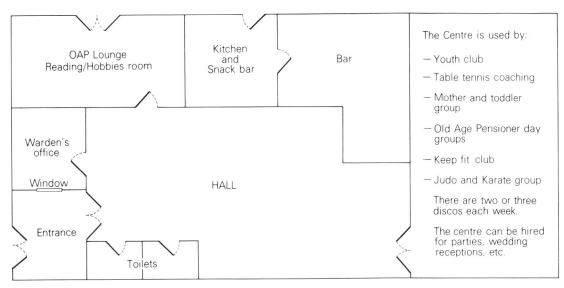

This Community Centre had a fixed Payphone in the entrance porch. One night the Payphone was vandalised. The Warden thought it would be a good idea to have one portable Payphone on a trolley and several sockets in various parts of the Community Centre.

1 Draw or trace the plan of the Community Centre.
2 Decide where you would put the Payphone sockets.
3 Put a clear mark on your plan to show exactly where each socket would be.
4 What are the advantages of having a portable Payphone in a Centre like this?
   Make a list of the advantages. Include in your list any special advantages for the groups using the centre. For example, the Old Age Pensioners would benefit from a Payphone in their lounge. Why?
5 You go to the Community Centre quite often.
   Write a letter to a friend. Tell your friend about the vandalising of the old Payphone and about the new portable Payphone. Explain to your friend how it is portable, where the sockets are and what people are saying about it.

Have your work marked.

ANSWERS **How to use the Payphone** Questions on page 85.

2   4   1   3

Inventions for people with special needs

A telephone you can dial with your mouth

A firm called Possum Controls Limited makes electronic control equipment for severely handicapped and severely disabled people.

In this photograph you can see a man using the Possum Selector Unit, the *PSU* 3. This system includes an indicator panel which shows the many electrical appliances controlled by the *PSU* 3.

One electrical appliance the *PSU* 3 can control is the telephone. The *PSU* 3 can give full dialling control over a loudspeaking telephone.

When the man wants to use the system he presses the microswitch or sucks or puffs on the tube. This causes a light on the indicator panel to travel downwards from the "start" position and then across the indicator panel. In this way, he can select just what he wants on the indicator panel.

Beginnings and endings

WRITING Read the beginnings of eight sentences on the left. The endings to these sentences are in the wrong order. Match the beginnings with the right endings then write out each sentence in full.

BEGINNINGS

1 Possum Controls Limited is a firm

2 The man in the photograph
3 The many electrical appliances controlled by the Possum Selector Unit
4 Full dialling control over a loudspeaking telephone
5 The system can be operated
6 The light on the indicator panel

ENDINGS

A can be given by a Possum Selector Unit.
B by gentle puffing or sucking on a tube.
C which makes special electronic control equipment.
D travels down and then across the panel.

E are shown on an indicator panel.
F is using the Possum Selector Unit, the *PSU* 3.

Turn to page 93 for the answers.

ANSWERS **Choose the right word** Questions on pages 83–84:

1 you	19 ring	36 until
2 advertised	20 shop	37 sold
3 night	21 kilometres	38 one
4 buy	22 here	39 want
5 cameras	23 information	40 give
6 camera	24 shop	41 (your name & address)
7 number	25 camera	42 Thursday
8 Thank	26 ask	43 park
9 Goodbye	27 any	44 Centre
10 Tele	28 idea	45 car
11 know	29 Hello	46 cross
12 buy	30 help	47 shop
13 television	31 camera	48 forgot
14 type	32 electronic	49 on
15 built-in	33 lens	50 thought/expected
16 telephoto	34 arrived	51 see
17 camera	35 like	52 Thursday
18 available		

Inventing a car for Terry

READING Terry Wiles was born without arms or legs. He did have deformed feet with toes on them. When he was nearly nine years old and only 53 centimetres tall, he was adopted by Leonard and Hazel Wiles. Leonard wanted to encourage Terry to develop the natural movement he had in his shoulders and his deformed feet. He thought that a wheelchair car with a lift mechanism would help Terry. Terry could move himself into this at floor level and then press a control lever with his shoulder to move himself up to normal height.

Read this extract from the Terry Wiles story. The name of the book is *On Giant's Shoulders*.

Terry needed not only to lift himself a few inches from the ground, but to meet people at their own level, to look into their eyes, to work at table height. The disadvantage of being twenty-one inches (53 centimetres) tall was living in a world where everything and everybody had to be looked up to.

But Terry did not only need to have his eyes at the right level. He needed to be able to "stoop": to lower himself to the floor to pick up a dropped knife, to rise to place it on the table, or higher still to reach a shelf or paint a door frame. Leonard wanted to make a mechanical extension of Terry's tiny body which simply lifted him to wherever he wanted to be as quickly and easily as possible.

Leonard looked at the hydraulic jack used in garages to whisk cars off their wheels. It was fast enough, but expensive, difficult to control and might leak oil on the carpets. That was not for Supercar, he decided. No, the answer was a fork-lift truck designed to lift crates, bales or barrels. He looked at the way the machine was built.

Supercar was built from a bicycle chain, powered by a pair of windscreen motors, and fitted with a comfortable bucket seat for Terry.

In January 1972, the four winter months of self-denial were rewarded: Leonard was able to bring the Supercar into the cottage for its first major test in the living room. Apart from a final coat of paint, here it was – ready. Terry and Hazel had faith in Leonard's skill, but they wondered if Supercar could really do all that Leonard said it would.

There the machine stood, tall and out of place in the living room. Leonard and Hazel pushed the sofa and armchairs back against the walls, leaving Terry a clear area.

"Now we sit down," Leonard told Hazel, "and let Terry do the work."

"I can start now, Daddy?"

Leonard nodded. Terry slid on to the seat, which lay at ground level.

"Now the safety-belt: you know what to do." Using his teeth and shoulder, Terry strung over the safety-belt. He was still looking up at them.

"Away you go."

Grinning nervously, Terry leaned against the vertical control with his shoulder. Smoothly the seat moved up and up. The floorboards fell away from Terry, and the toys he had left to one side. Suddenly he was afraid.

"Keep going. You won't fall off the top." Heart thudding, Terry maintained the pressure, and the chair continued to rise. He was now on a level with his parents' eyes . . . he was going higher still. He was above Hazel's head! The seat came to rest.

There was a moment's silence. Hazel and Leonard looked up at him, Hazel in wonderment, and Leonard with pride.

"Go to the table."

The agile toes tightened on the tiny control column. Supercar began to rotate, then move forwards, smoothly, towards the table. Terry's feet were level with the tabletop. He turned to look at them, face alight:

"I don't need help any more! I can get here myself and I can feed myself!"

Interviews

WRITING You have been given the chance of talking to Terry and his parents. Before you go to see them you make a list of the questions you would like to ask them. Write out these questions and then add two or three to each section.

Questions for Hazel
1 What made you and Leonard decide to adopt Terry?
2 You had to do without things during the four winter months that Leonard was making the Supercar. What were the things you did without and what did you miss the most?

Questions for Leonard
1 Why did you want to build a Supercar for Terry?
2 What gave you the idea of a seat that goes from floor level upwards?

Questions for Terry
1 How did you move about before you had the Supercar?
2 What difference does the Supercar make to your life now?

1 Decide who is going to be Terry, Hazel, Leonard and the visitor. The visitor starts a conversation with the Wiles family, using the prepared questions.

2 WRITING Write the story of Terry's first journey out of the house on his own in his new Supercar. Pretend you are Terry himself.

Have your work marked.

ANSWERS **Three reasons for having a Payphone** Definitions on page 86.

1 C   2 A   3 E   4 G   5 B   6 H   7 F   8 D

ANSWERS **Beginnings and endings** Questions on page 89.

1 C   2 F   3 E   4 A   5 B   6 D

Amusing solution

Jo collects interesting and unusual photographs. Here is one which she was pleased to have in her collection.

1 Why do you think Jo chose this photograph for her collection?
   What is interesting or amusing about it?
2 What is unusual about the spectacles? How do they work?
3 Why do you think the spectacles were made?
4 Write a story called *The Most Amusing Invention*, in which you tell the story behind this picture.
5 Design and write an advertisement for this invention. Include information on different designs, advantages of wearing this product, details of how it works, the cost and the guarantee.

Have your work marked.

5 Word perfect

Title, title page, contents and index

WRITING Look at the drawing of the book. Answer these questions.

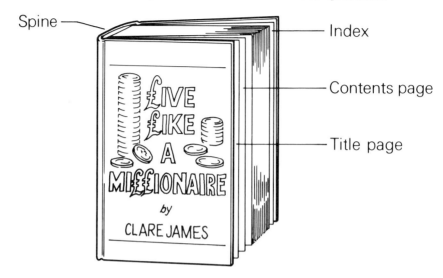

1 What is the title of the book?
2 Who wrote this book?
3 The writer of a book is called an _____.
4 Whereabouts in the book is the page marked "Contents"?
5 Is the Index at the back or the front of this book?

The answers are on page 99.

Words and definitions

Here is a definition of a title page: the page at the front of a book giving the title, writer's name, etc.

Now read these five definitions and sort out the right word order for each one. Then write down the words and their correct definitions.

1 title   a book, painting/given to/the name/play, etc
2 contents   the front/of chapters/found at/of a book/a list
3 index   at the back of a book/and the pages where they can be found/of names, subjects, etc, mentioned in it/an alphabetical list
4 chapter   divisions of a book/has a number/which usually/or a title/one of the main
5 etc   and the rest, and so on/a shortened form/which means/of et cetera

The answers are on page 105.

Match title and contents

WRITING On the *RIGHT* are four lists of Contents from four books. On the *LEFT* are the four titles of these books in the wrong order. Match the right title with each list of contents then write out the *titles* in the correct order.

TITLES	*CONTENTS*	
Live Like a Millionaire	1 Famous Buildings in Woodstead	page 1
	2 Interesting Walks and Tours	page 12
	3 Sport for All	page 25
	4 A Choice of Entertainment	page 34
Longman New Generation Dictionary	1 Headline news	page 5
	2 Sending messages	page 29
	3 Planning a holiday	page 53
	4 Invention and communication	page 73
	5 Word perfect	page 95
	Index	page 110
Woodstead A Guide for Tourists	1 How to start your own business	page 1
	2 Investing your money wisely	page 22
	3 Best buys at sales and auctions	page 40
	4 Bargain clothes that will impress people	page 56
	5 A night out that won't cost a fortune	page 72
	Index	page 81
Day to Day English	Guide to the Dictionary	inside front cover
	Using your Dictionary	page 6a
	Preface	page 12a
	Acknowledgments	page 15a
	The Dictionary	page 1
	Word Parts	page 784
	Spelling Table	page 787
	Foreign Alphabets	page 789
	List of Illustrations	inside back cover

The answers are on page 105.

A dictionary has a contents but no index

WRITING Look again at the contents page of the *Longman New Generation Dictionary* on page 97. Answer these questions.

1 Which page would you turn to to find out how to make full use of the Dictionary?
2 Where would you find a list of illustrations in the dictionary?
3 Which page gives you information about spelling?
4 What is the meaning of these two words (*a*) Preface
(*b*) Acknowledgement?

The list of contents shows you at a glance what is contained in the *Dictionary*. The list of contents also saves you time by showing you what page to turn to to find this information. Look again at the definition of *Index* on page 96. Answer this question.

5 Why is there no index at the back of a dictionary?

The answers are on page 105.

Finding a word in a dictionary

READING The words in a dictionary are arranged in alphabetical order. This means that if you want to look up **breakdown** you look among the words beginning with **b.** Many words begin with **b** so look next at the second letter of breakdown which is **r.** Words beginning with **br** come after the **bo** words like **boyfriend** and before the **bu** words like **bubble.** But there are a lot of **br** words so look next at the third letter which is **e.** Words beginning **bre** come after words such as **brace** but before words like **bridge.** Next look at the fourth letter which is **a**, and then the fifth letter and so on until you come to **breakdown.**

How quickly can you find a word?

Work with a friend who has a watch with a seconds counter. One of you has a closed dictionary. The other writes out these six words clearly on separate pieces of paper.

criminal	jeweller	steal
security	midnight	window

The one with the dictionary is given any one of the six words. While the word is being found in the dictionary, the friend counts the seconds. Take turns until you have both found all six words. Add up the total number of seconds each one took to find the six words in the dictionary.

How quickly can you fill in the missing letters?

WRITING All the words on the left begin with **break-** or **safe-**. The boxes show the shape of the missing letters. Read the definition opposite each word and work out the missing letters. Write down the full version of each word. Do not write out the definition. Look up "Wordshapes" in the index at the end of this book.

1 break ⬚⬚⬚ a sudden failure in a machine, engine, etc which causes it to stop working properly.

2 break ⬚⬚⬚⬚ to do business without making either a profit or a loss.

3 break ⬚⬚⬚ the first meal of the day.

4 break- ⬚⬚ the unlawful entering of a building, using force.

5 break ⬚⬚⬚⬚ very fast or dangerous.

6 safe ⬚⬚⬚⬚⬚ a thief who breaks into safes.

7 safe- ⬚⬚⬚⬚⬚⬚ safe storing of valuable objects, usually in small boxes in a bank.

8 safe ⬚⬚ freedom from danger, harm or risk.

9 safe ⬚⬚·⬚⬚⬚ a strap fastened around a person sitting in a seat (as in a car or aeroplane) for safety.

10 safe ⬚⬚ ⬚⬚⬚⬚ a part of a machine which allows gas, steam, etc, to escape when the pressure is too great.

The answers are on page 105.

ANSWERS **Title, title page, contents and index** Question on page 96.

1 *Live Like a Millionaire*
2 Clare James
3 Author
4 In the front, after the Title Page
5 At the back

Encyclopedias

An encyclopedia has its contents on its spine

READING Sort out this dictionary definition.

encyclopedia   in alphabetical order/a book or set of books/or with one particular branch/dealing with every branch of knowledge.

Check your answer with a dictionary.

ABBEY TO CALYPSO Volume 1	CAMEL TO ELASTIC Volume 2	ELBOW TO GOLD Volume 3	GOLF TO INDIA Volume 4	INDIGO TO LUNG Volume 5	LUPIN TO NUT Volume 6
NYLON TO PUTTY Volume 7	PUZZLE TO RIVER Volume 8	RIVET TO TOMATO Volume 9	TOMB IO WAVE Volume 10	WAX TO ZULU Volume 11	INDEX & MAPS Volume 12

The contents of an encyclopedia, like the contents of a dictionary, are arranged in alphabetical order. So in Volume 1 you would find information on abbeys, America, bank, bridge, calories, calypso and many more things. The words on the spine show the first item (Abbey) and the last item (Calypso) in that volume. Inside the encyclopedia you will find information on all the items between these two words arranged in alphabetical order.

Find the right volume

WRITING In which volume would you find information on these items? Write down the answers.

1 denim	6 insect	11 football	16 ski
2 judo	7 quicksand	12 lynx	17 pearls
3 pyramid	8 canal	13 umbrella	18 zodiac
4 glider	9 valve	14 Bible	19 horse
5 roller-skate	10 oil	15 xylophone	20 mascot

The answers are on page 105.

Match the items

READING Sometimes an encyclopedia does not seem to have the information you want, because the word or item you look up is not there. For example, you may want to find out about how to take good pictures. So you look up pictures but the information in the encyclopedia is about paintings and art galleries. So you look up photograph. There is no information on photograph but there is a long section on PHOTOGRAPHY. In this section you read about how to take good pictures and also about cameras, film, developing and printing. Here are a few more examples.

LIST A	LIST B
The information you want	*The section where you will find it*
songs, bands, records	MUSIC
hockey, football, tennis	SPORT
flying	AEROPLANE
clothes	FASHION

WRITING Match the items in *LIST C* with the correct sections in *LIST D*. Write down the numbers *1* to *10* on separate lines on a piece of paper. These numbers represent the items in *LIST C*. Next to each number put the correct section from *LIST D*. The answer to number *1* is *FOOD*.

LIST C	LIST D
Items	*Sections in the encyclopedia*
1 rice, vegetables, protein	SAILING
2 art	WEAPONS
3 budgerigar, gerbil, goldfish	MAKE-UP
4 vehicle	FOOD
5 carburettor, sparking plug, piston	ASTROLOGY
6 eye shadow, lipstick	TRANSPORT
7 rocket, satellite	PETS
8 yacht, catamaran, dinghy	PAINTING
9 zodiac	SPACECRAFT
10 gun, rifle, sword	ENGINE

Now, next to each section you have written down, write the number of the volume where you would find information on it. For example, information on *FOOD* would be found in Volume 3.

The answers are on page 107.

A map has an index but no contents list

READING Every map showing a detailed street plan of a town has a street index. This index is printed either at the side or at the bottom of the map and it is in alphabetical order. After each street in the index there is a letter and a number. For example, Kingswood Road C4.

Look at this map to see what the letter and the number mean.

1 Find letter C at the top of the map. Any street or road marked C in the index will be somewhere in column C on the map.

2 Find number 4 at the right hand side of the map. Any street or road marked 4 in the index will be in this column of the map.

Where C and 4 meet is square C4 which is where you will find Kingswood Road.

Abbreviations used on maps

To save space on the map some words are shortened or abbreviated. Here is a list of abbreviations which are used on maps.

Ave. – Avenue	Gro. – Grove	Sq. – Square
Clo. – Close	La. – Lane	St. – Street
Cres. – Crescent	Pk. – Park	Ter. – Terrace
Dr. – Drive	Pl. – Place	Wk. – Walk
Gdns. – Gardens	Rd. – Road	Wy. – Way

Make your own street index

1 **WRITING** Arrange this list of streets, roads, etc into alphabetical order. Write out the names of the roads in full.

Willow Gdns.	Oakwood Wy.
Beech Cres.	Elm Dr.
Forest Gro.	Market Pl.
Meadow Clo.	Linden La.
Canal Wk.	Kingswood Rd.
Locksway Ave.	Duke St.

2 After each road, street, etc, write down the correct letter and number so that it can be found quickly on the map.

The answers are on page 107.

WOODSTEAD

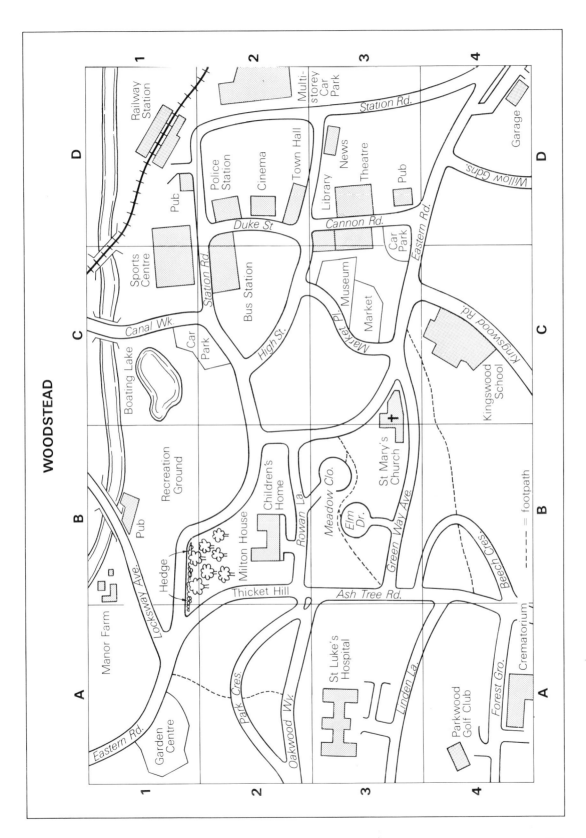

Moving into Woodstead

Piu Yun moved into Greenway Ave., Woodstead, a month ago. At the end of the month Piu Yun wrote to her friend in Milton Keynes. The letter included this information:

1 What the new house was like.
2 How her room had been decorated.
3 What new friends she had made.
4 What she liked about Woodstead
　eg sport, cinema, disco, shops, etc.
5 An invitation to come and stay for a weekend.
6 Directions to 2 Greenway Ave. from the Bus Station.

The full address is 2 Greenway Avenue, Woodstead, Derbyshire. Write a reply to Piu Yun's letter from the friend.

Have your work marked.

Using the Yellow Pages in Woodstead

WRITING Piu Yun's family need to know the telephone numbers of some local shops and services. They make a list of the ones they want. Put this list into alphabetical order. Write down each one on a separate line.

LIST A

Pet shops	Florists	Hairdressers
Dry cleaning	Launderettes	Wine and spirits
Newsagents	Bakers	Jewellers

Here is a list of nine local shop names or business names. Find one for each of the shops you have just put into alphabetical order. After the name of the shop from *LIST A*, write the matching name and telephone number from *LIST B*.

LIST B

Wash Tub, The	Woodstead 55403
Animal Care	Beechgrove 71246
Earrings "n" Things	Oakwood 33524
Bottle and Jug, The	Woodstead 51681
Rainbow Flower Shop	Beechgrove 71618
Instant Cleaners	Oakwood 35607
P and J News	Woodstead 55462
Bread Bin, The	Oakwood 37825
Marcus Hair Fashions	Beechgrove 71768

Words and definitions Question on page 96.

1 title   the name given to a book, painting, play, etc.
2 contents a list of chapters found at the front of a book.
3 index   an alphabetical list at the back of a book of names, subjects, etc,
           mentioned in it and the pages where they can be found.
4 chapter   one of the main divisions of a book which usually has a number or a title.
5 etc   a shortened form of et cetera which means and the rest, and so on.

Match title and contents Questions on page 97.

1 *Woodstead – A Guide for Tourists*
2 *Day to Day English*
3 *Live like a Millionaire*
4 *Longman New Generation Dictionary*

A dictionary has a contents but no index Questions on page 98.

1 Page 6a
2 Inside back cover
3 Page 787
4 (a) an introduction to a book or speech
  (b) something given, done, said or printed in a book as a way of thanking.
5 As the words with their definitions are already in alphabetical order, a reader
  only has to follow the alphabetical order to find a word. There is no need for an
  index. In a sense, the dictionary is its own index.

Find the missing letters Questions on page 99.

1 breakdown   2 break even   3 breakfast   4 break-in
5 breakneck   6 safe breaker   7 safe-deposit   8 safety
9 safety-belt   10 safety valve

Find the right volume Questions on page 100.

1 Vol. 2   6 Vol. 5   11 Vol. 3   16 Vol. 9
2 Vol. 5   7 Vol. 8   12 Vol. 6   17 Vol. 7
3 Vol. 8   8 Vol. 2   13 Vol. 10   18 Vol. 11
4 Vol. 3   9 Vol. 10   14 Vol. 1   19 Vol. 4
5 Vol. 9   10 Vol. 7   15 Vol. 11   20 Vol. 6

Problems and protests in Woodstead

Road Safety problem – accident blackspot

READING Here are two accidents which took place on Eastern Road in Woodstead in the area where Locksway Avenue and Thicket Hill join Eastern Road. There is a 40 mph speed limit on this section of road.

Accident 1 A motorist in a Ford Cortina drove down Thicket Hill. He looked right quickly before beginning to turn left into Eastern Road. He could not see much of Eastern Road on his right because of the bend and the high hedge. As he pulled out into Eastern Road, a large furniture van coming from the centre of Woodstead crashed into the car. The van was travelling at 45 mph.

Accident 2 A minibus turned left at the end of Locksway Avenue into Eastern Road. The minibus had to go wide at the corner in order to get round it because Locksway Avenue is fairly narrow and at an awkward angle where it joins Eastern Road. As the minibus went wide of the corner, it crossed the centre of the road. A Vauxhall Chevette travelling at 40 mph coming from Woodstead had to move out to avoid a cyclist who had come down Thicket Hill too fast. The cyclist had swerved left into Eastern Road. The car and the minibus crashed into each other.

WRITING Answer these questions. Look back at the map of Woodstead.

Accident 1
1 How could the driver of the Ford Cortina have avoided the crash?
2 Was the furniture van driver to blame in any way?
3 What could be done to make this junction safer?

Accident 2
4 Who is most to blame and who is least to blame for this accident?
5 What could be done to make a left turn from Locksway Avenue into Eastern Road safer for drivers?

Both accidents
6 What road signs, speed restrictions or road markings or any other improvements would you suggest to prevent accidents like this happening on this part of Eastern Road?
7 Draw a map showing the changes you would make to make this section of road as safe as possible.

Have your work marked.

Public protest – Save our recreation ground

READING The Woodstead Town Council have announced that they are going to close the Recreation Ground, its Car Park and fill in the Boating Lake. This is going to be done so that the Council can build fifty houses in this area.

The people who live in the town, the residents, form an action committee to organise a protest against the decision to build the houses on the Recreation Ground.

Here are some of the things they decide to do.

1 To organise a letter of protest to the Town Council.
2 To hold a public meeting in the Cinema or Theatre.
3 To advertise the protest campaign in the local newspaper.
4 To organise a protest march.

WRITING

1 Write the letter to the Town Council explaining why you oppose their plans.
2 Write a newspaper report about the public meeting or the protest march.
3 Design a full-page advertisement for the local paper.

Have your work marked.

ANSWERS **Match the items** Questions on page 101.

1 FOOD Vol. 3
2 PAINTING Vol. 7
3 PETS Vol. 7
4 TRANSPORT Vol. 10
5 ENGINE Vol. 3
6 MAKE-UP Vol. 6
7 SPACECRAFT Vol. 9
8 SAILING Vol. 9
9 ASTROLOGY Vol. 1
10 WEAPONS Vol. 11

ANSWERS **Make your own street index** Questions on page 102.

Beech Crescent	B4	Linden Lane	A3
Canal Walk	C1	Locksway Avenue	B1
Duke Street	D2	Market Place	C3
Elm Drive	B3	Meadow Close	B3
Forest Grove	A4	Oakwood Way	A2
Kingswood Road	C4	Willow Gardens	D4

Campaign pictures?

WRITING Look carefully at these photographs. They could be linked with a protest campaign or a safety campaign. Write down a list of possible links. Choose the most interesting idea from each list and write a story to go with each photograph.

Have your work marked.

Index

Note: dictionary definitions are taken from the Longman New Generation Dictionary

Acknowledgements

We are grateful to Times Books for permission to reproduce adapted extracts from *On Giant's Shoulders* by Marjorie Wallace and Michael Robson, 1976.

We are grateful to the following for permission to reproduce photographs: *Daily Telegraph*, page 67; Dennis Dobson, page 11; Keith Fletcher, pages 18 and 19; *The Guardian*, page 108; Kobal Collection, page 25 (from Avco Embassy Pictures film *The Fog*, directed by John Carpenter); Lugger Hotel, Portloe, Truro, page 57 left; Mansell Collection, page 76; David Parker, page 6;   Possum Controls Ltd, Langley, page 88; Press Association, page 22; John Roan, page 16 above; *Sunday Times*, page 74 (photo Sally Soames); Syndication International/*Daily Mirror*, pages 94 and 109; *The Times*. page 66; Times Books, page 91; Trusthouse Forte Hotels/New Bath Hotel, Matlock Bath page 57 right; Janine Wiedel, page 104. Photographs on page 16 below left by Bob Barrett; page 16 below right by Longman Photographic Unit.

Facsimile newspaper articles are reproduced with the permission of; Associated Newspapers Group/*Evening News*, page 6; Associated Press/*Daily Telegraph*, page 26; *The Guardian*, page 22.
The application form for a British Visitor's Passport is Crown copyright and reproduced on page 62 with the permission of the Controller of Her Majesty's Stationery Office. The map on page 33 has been adapted with the permission of Stevenage Borough Council.